OpenOffice.org Calc

Functions and Formulas

Tips

OpenOffice.org Calc Functions and Formulas Tips

Essential OpenOffice.org Calc Formula Skills

by

Jacek Artymiak

First Edition

London 2010

OpenOffice.org Calc Functions and Formulas Tips, 1st ed.
by Jacek Artymiak

Published by devGuide.net ltd

www: http://www.devguide.net/openoffice

email: ooocfaft1@devguide.net

First edition 2010

Printed in Poland and the United States of America.

10 10 9 8 7 6 5 4 3 2 1

ISBN: 978-83-60869-23-9

Table of Contents

List of Tables

Introduction

Functions and formulas are the secret weapon in every spreadsheet user's arsenal. They help you quickly analyze huge amount of data or build interactive models that let you try different scenarios before you commit your time and money to a project. If you ever wanted to compare prices, financing options, or find out when you are going to break even, you should be using formulas to make such analysis as easy as punching different numbers into the spreadsheet.

I wrote this book to help you quickly learn how to use functions and formulas in OpenOffice.org Calc. It is not a long book, because I want you to get up to speed as fast as possible.

I hope you will find this book a valuable resource.

Jacek Artymiak
London, January 2010

Chapter 1

Essentials

In this chapter you will learn the basics of working with data in OpenOffice.org Calc—how to enter, edit, organize, and format information.

☞ To get the best out of the information presented in this book, especially when you are just beginning to learn OpenOffice.org Calc, you might want to create a new worksheet to experiment with the tools and the techniques described on the following pages.

☞ To help you learn faster, we have prepared a companion worksheet that you can download from:

http://www.devguide.net/openoffice

Creating a New Worksheet

You can create a new worksheet in a number of ways, but selecting **File ⇨ New ⇨ Spreadsheet** is probably the most convenient way of doing it from any OpenOffice.org module. (See Figure 1.1 on the next page.)

☞ Pressing **Ctrl+N** is also a handy shortcut when you already are working in OpenOffice.org Calc.

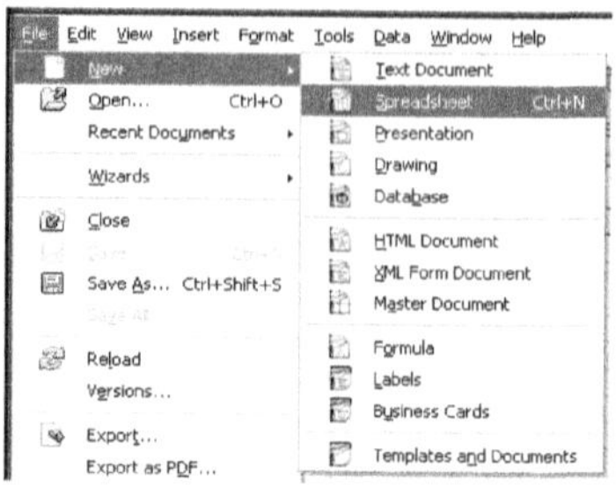

Figure 1.1: Creating a new worksheet.

Entering Data

Entering information into an OpenOffice.org Calc worksheet is generally a matter of double-clicking on a cell and typing whatever it is you wish to type. A single hit on the **Enter/Return** key stores your input inside the current cell.

- Pressing one of the cursor (arrows) keys on the keyboard or clicking on another cell has the same effect unless you are entering a formula, in which case OpenOffice.org Calc will insert references to the cells you moved the spreadsheet cursor to. To get out of that mode, press **Esc**.
- The spreadsheet cursor is the thick, black frame around a cell. The text cursor is the black, vertical bar that moves across the screen as you type.

OpenOffice.org Calc is smart enough to recognize a lot of popular types of data (numbers, money, dates, text, etc.). Whatever you type into a cell appears inside that cell and on the **Input Line** field located at the top of the worksheet area.

- The **Input Line** is a useful feedback tool. If something doesn't look right inside a cell, the **Input Line** will always show you its raw, unformatted content.
- The **Input Line** is also a convenient place to edit data.
- To edit data stored inside a cell do any of the following actions: double-click on it, press **F2**, or click once on the **Input Line**.

Figure 1.2: The Input Line (the field in the top right corner) is both a feedback window and a cell editing field.

How OpenOffice.org Calc Treats Your Input

OpenOffice.org Calc uses an elaborate set of rules to determine how to classify and display the information you store inside a worksheet. Most of those rules are fairly straightforward and as long as you properly set the operating system's local settings for date and money formatting, whatever you type or paste ought to be interpreted in the right way.

The following sections explain how OpenOffice.org Calc treats each type of data. Read them if you want to understand why your input is being interpreted, displayed, and printed the way it is. You will also pick up tips on forcing OpenOffice.org Calc to interpret your input in the way you think is right.

Text

Entering text into a cell is as straightforward as it can possibly be. Just double-click on a cell, type whatever you want to type, then hit the **Enter/Return** key.

OpenOffice.org Calc is smart enough to tell apart dates, formulas, numbers, text, and time. When it gets confused and does not understand your input one way or another it will treat what you type as text. For example, `Annual Report`, `Year 2010 Sales in Omaha`, `1st Quarter Results`, or `2010 Sales Summary` are all treated as text.

> You can force OpenOffice.org Calc to treat any kind of input as a string of text by placing a single quote (`'`) in front of it. Type `1000` and `'1000` into two separate cells to see the difference for yourself. (See Figure 1.3 on the next page.)

Figure 1.3: Forcing numbers to be treated as text.

Numbers

Numbers are a bit more complex to handle. If you ever get confused by the way OpenOffice.org Calc interprets your input, here is a list of rules that will help you understand what is happening:

- If you enter anything that resembles a number, it will be interpreted as you would expect. So `1000`, `1.23`, and `1.44444` are all stored and displayed as ordinary integer or floating-point (fractional) numbers.

- Any number preceded by the dollar sign (`$`) is treated as a currency value and will be formatted using the currency style. So `$1000000` will be displayed as `$1,000,000.00`. (Styles and formatting are discussed later in Chapter 4 on page 27.)

- You can separate thousands with the comma sign (`,`), as in `1,000,000`, but not with a period (`.`) which is reserved for the decimal point. Numbers with commas, but without the dollar sign in front of them, are displayed as ordinary numbers—the commas will be removed, the decimal point will stay in its place. This behavior varies depending on the regional settings, some counties use periods (`.`) to separate thousands and commas (`,`) to indicate the decimal point.

- A number followed by the percent sign (`%`) is treated as a percentage value. For example, `10.25%` is shown exactly as you typed it in, which is useful if you do not have the time to convert percentages to their fractional equivalents.

- It is OK to use common fractions. You see these numbers fairly often if you work with or invest in securities, there is no reason you should not be able to use them. Remember to put a space between the integer part and the fraction, as in 12 3/4. Use the slash sign (/) to separate the numerator from the denominator.

- Whenever you enter a common fraction, OpenOffice.org Calc turns it into a decimal fraction to speed up internal calculations. Don't worry. The cell that stores the original input will still display it as a common fraction. The **Input Line** shows the fraction after conversion.
- You can change the number of decimal places shown in cells. You will find the necessary information in Chapter 4 on page 33.
- Scientific exponential notation, such as 10e12 or -27.4567e-45, is permitted.
- Placing the minus sign (-) in front of a number turns it into a negative number.
- For more information about the precision of calculations, see the "Numeric Formats" section in Chapter 4 on page 32.
- For more tips on formatting numbers, see the "Formatting Text and Numbers" see the "Numeric Formats" section in Chapter 4 on page 32.

Dates

Series of numbers separated with a slash (/), a period (.), or a hyphen (-) are treated as calendar dates, if they fall within certain limits (see Chapter 12, "Time and Date Functions" on page 121).

For example, 12/29/2010, 12.29.2010, and 12-29-2010 are all interpreted by OpenOffice.org Calc as December 29, 2000, but 12-000/23/19345, will be interpreted as text.

- To force OpenOffice.org Calc to interpret the numbers that look like calendar dates as text, put a single quote (') in front of the number, .e.g. type '12/29/2010 instead of 12/29/2010.
- Date formatting for display depends on the operating system's local settings. Internally, the dates you enter are stored in the same format.

Figure 1.4: Editing text stored inside a cell.

It is a good idea to get used to typing the year in dates as a four digit number and not as the commonly used two-digit number. This prevents subtle errors caused by the computer misinterpreting dates.

Time

Any series of numbers separated with one or two colons (`:`) will be interpreted as a time value. For example, `12:13` is displayed as `12:13:00`. Similarly, `9:4:34` is displayed as `9:04:34`. You can even enter `9582:3566:23445345` and OpenOffice.org Calc will convert it into the proper number of hours, minutes and seconds, but `2:432:7:33` (notice the third colon) is assumed to represent a string of text. Minutes and seconds are always displayed as two-digit numbers.

If you want to prevent OpenOffice.org Calc from automatically interpreting what you entered as a time value, place a single quote (`'`) in front of the time string, as in `'97:45:18`.

Editing Data

We all make mistakes. Not necessarily because we are careless, but because working with numbers is a rather boring affair and there are plenty of opportunities to introduce errors. Fortunately, they can be easily corrected at any time.

Correcting or changing the content of a worksheet is called *editing*. You can tell that you are in the editing mode when you see a text cursor inside the current cell and its content "spills" over to the neighboring cells (see Figure 1.4).

Here are a few tips on editing data in OpenOffice.org Calc:

- To enter the edit mode, select a cell using the mouse or the keyboard cursor keys and then either double-click on it or press **F2**.
- You can move about inside a cell using the **Left** and **Right** keyboard cursor keys.
- The **Up** and **Down** cursor keys should not be used as they move the spreadsheet cursor (the thick, black rectangular frame) to the cell above or below the current one.
- Press **Shift** + ⇦ or **Shift** + ⇨ to select a portion of the cell's content. Press **Ctrl+A** to select all of it.
- Use **Ctrl+C**, **Ctrl+X**, and **Ctrl+V** to copy, cut, and paste the selected content.
- Use the **Ctrl+Enter** keyboard shortcut to insert line breaks.
- The **Enter/Return** key is used to end the cell edit mode and store the changes you have made inside the current cell.
- If you want to abandon all of your changes while you are still in the edit mode, press **Esc**.
- Undoing recent changes after you hit the **Enter/Return** key is done in the usual way, with the **Ctrl+Z** keyboard shortcut.
- When you are editing long pieces of text or complex formulas, you might want to do your edits on the **Input Line** (located above the active sheet). It will be more comfortable than editing inside the cell itself.

Adding Comments to Cells

A well-designed worksheet ought to be self-explanatory and you should not need to add a lot of extra comments to it, but there are plenty of situations when you want to add additional information not meant to be visible when you print or show your data to others.

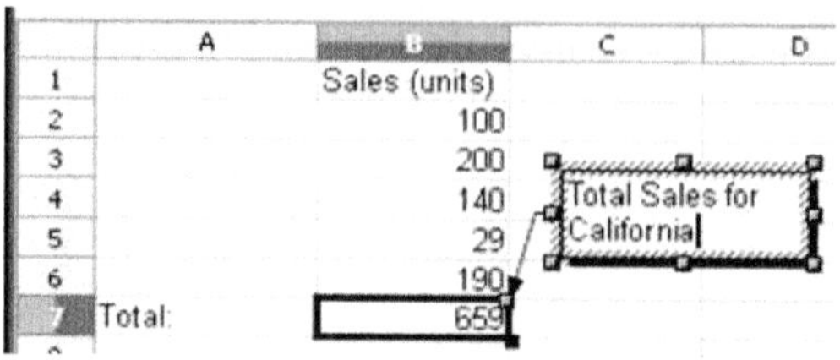

Figure 1.5: The OpenOffice.org Calc version of the famous yellow sticky notes.

Things like "Call me when the client asks for a discount bigger than 10%" are a good examples of notes that you should add as hidden notes. OpenOffice.org Calc lets you add notes to any cell. It's really simple.

- Choose **Insert ⇨ Notes**, which opens a yellow rectangular box where you can type short comments regarding that particular cell (see Figure 1-5).
- A cell with a note has a tiny red square in the top-right corner.
- When you want to see the note attached to a cell, right-click on the cell with the note and choose **Show Note**.
- Switching to the note editing mode is simply a matter of clicking on it when it is visible on the screen.
- To delete the note, right-click on the cell with the note and choose **Delete Note**.

Chapter 2

Formulas

In this chapter you are going to learn how to write OpenOffice.org Calc formulas. Formulas are simple, yet powerful tools that let you create smart documents which automatically update themselves without too much human intervention. This may sound like rocket science, but it's actually very simple.

Once you understand how formulas works, it really is a great joy to be able to build a complex document that does all the math for you while you focus on solving the real problem.

A Short Guide to Writing Great Formulas

No matter what it does, every formula starts with the equals sign (=). A formula can be as simple as a reference to another cell, for example, `=A4` placed in any cell other than A4 copies the value of A4 into that cell.

☞ Formulas can be even simpler. For example, `=7` is a formula too! But it is not very useful.

Understanding Formula Syntax

OpenOffice.org Calc formulas look and behave a lot like the equations you learned in your math classes, only the equals sign (=) is on the left hand side of the equation, rather than the more "natural" right hand side.

All of the standard mathematical operators are available for your perusal and they look and work just as in any other spreadsheet or math software. Their names and symbols are as follows:

- Addition (+)
- Subtraction (-)
- Multiplication (*)
- Division (/)
- Exponentiation (^)

OpenOffice.org Calc follows the standard mathematical order of operations: exponentiation, multiplication and division (from left to right), and addition and subtraction (from left to right).

- You can change the order of formula evaluation using parentheses as shown in the following examples:

  `=7+9*2^2`

  returns 43, while

  `=7+(9*2)^2`

  returns 331, and

  `=(7+9)*2^2`

  returns 64.

All parentheses must be matched—that is, any left parenthesis (must be matched by an appropriately placed right parenthesis).

Figure 2.1: How addressing and references work in practice. Cell A1 stores number 100, cell B1 stores the formula that references the contents of cell A1.

Referencing Cells

Typing all sorts of information into a worksheet is a good way to organize it, but that is all you can do with it. If you want to process that data, you need a way to reference the values stored inside cells and a notation that lets you express how you want to process those values.

Referencing cells and processing data is possible thanks to two powerful tools: *cell addressing* and *formulas*.

- Being able to reference other cells using their addresses lets you create formulas that update their results as soon as you finish editing the values they refer to.
- Any address inside a single sheet in a worksheet is made of two coordinates: a column number represented by a sequence of letters (e.g. AF) and an integer row number (e.g. `125`). Row numbers follow column numbers, e.g. `AF125`.
- A formula always begins with the equals sign (=) and can contain complex calculations described using a mixture of mathematical operators and OpenOffice.org Calc's built-in functions.
- You can use references to other cells as the arguments of OpenOffice.org Calc's functions.

The best way to see how addressing, references and formulas work in practice is by trying out a simple example (see Figure 2.1):

1. Type any number or text into any cell. Remember its address.

OpenOffice.org Calc displays the current cell's address on the toolbar in the drop-down box on the left. Column and row headers also change their color to give you visual cues.

2. Move the spreadsheet cursor to another cell.

3. Type the equals sign (=), followed by the original cell's address.

4. Press **Enter./Return**.

Note that OpenOffice.org Calc displays the same numeric values or text in both cells, even though they contain different kinds of information; the first cell contains raw information, while the second contains a reference to the first cell's contents.

Relative Addressing

The type of addressing used in the example in the previous section is called "relative," because of the way OpenOffice.org Calc treats such addresses when you decide to copy or move the cells that contain such references.

When you use relative addressing OpenOffice.org Calc will update the references to point to the cells located within the same relative distance ("two cells to the left, one cell up") to the relocated cells. How does it work in practice? Suppose you have a simple formula like `=A1` in cell B1. When you copy that formula from cell B1 to C1, OpenOffice.org Calc will automatically change it from `=A1` to `=B1`.

Any time you see an address made up of letters and digits only (e.g. `A1`) it is a relative address.

Absolute Addressing

OpenOffice.org Calc is smart, but it is not smart enough to guess when you'd rather not be using relative addressing. Automatic updates of addresses used in formulas are convenient, but not always welcome.

If you don't keep an eye on what is going on, relative addressing can lead to "unexplained" errors in calculations. For example, if you enter a number into cell A4, another number into A5, and a reference to A4 (=A4) into cell B4, and then copy the contents of B4 into B5, B5 displays the value of A5 instead of the value of A4. Depending on your needs, this might be good or bad. If you refer to a currency exchange table, you wouldn't necessarily want to switch from one currency to another. In such cases, you should use the "absolute" addressing notation. It bolts down cell references and tells OpenOffice.org Calc to leave them the way they are.

- To make sure that OpenOffice.org Calc leaves some addresses alone, put a dollar sign ($) in front of the column and the row parts of a cell's address. So, instead of typing `A4`, type `$A$4`. Once you do that, no matter where you copy your formula to it will always point to the right cell.

- You can use partial absolute addressing, such as `A$4` or `$A4` to limit absolute addressing to a particular column or row, if that's what you need.

- There is an easy way to change addresses from absolute to relative and back again. Select the cell in which you want to convert addresses and press **Shift+F4**. Pressing those keys repeatedly cycles through absolute rows, absolute columns, and relative rows and columns.

Referencing Data Stored on Other Sheets

You can write formulas that point to cells located on other sheets within the same worksheet document. All that you need to do is a small change of the target cell's address.

- If you want to reference cell B2 on sheet `California`, type `=California.B2`.

Referencing Data Stored in Other Worksheets

When you are referencing data held in other worksheets (separate spreadsheet document files), OpenOffice.org Calc needs some additional information to locate external files.

- When you reference cell B2 located on sheet `California` in worksheet USA, you need to type

  `='USA.ods'#$California.B2`

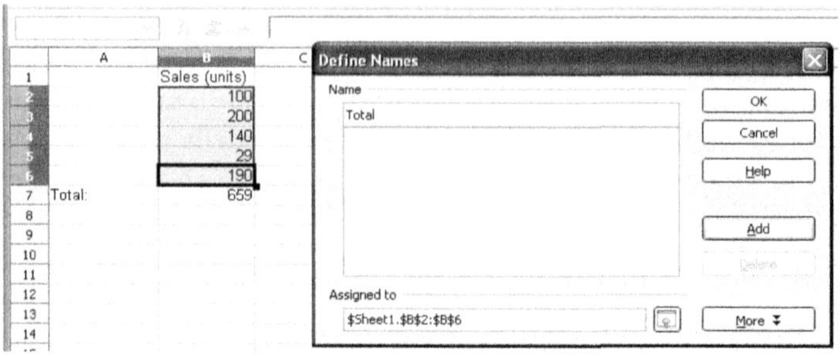

Figure 2.2: Naming blocks of cells.

The .ods suffix is used to complete the name of a worksheet created using OpenOffice.org Calc 3.1; other spreadsheets use different suffixes or no suffixes at all and you will have to adjust your references accordingly.

☞ The pound sign (#) and the dollar sign ($) in front of the name of the sheet are obligatory. They have no relation to absolute and relative addressing, although you can use both types of addressing in cell references, e.g.

```
='USA.ods'#$California.$B$2
```

☞ Filenames must be enclosed in single quotes (').

☞ If the worksheet you are referring to is not located in the same directory as the file that references it, you must give OpenOffice.org Calc a full path to that document, e.g.:

```
='/home/jack.white/monthly returns/customers/
USA.sdc'#$California.$B$2
```

The reference to the external file shown above is written in the style native to Linux and other Unix-like operating systems. On Microsoft Windows, it would look like this

```
='C:\Documents and Settings\Jack White\My
Documents\monthly returns\customers\USA.sdc'#
$California.B2
```

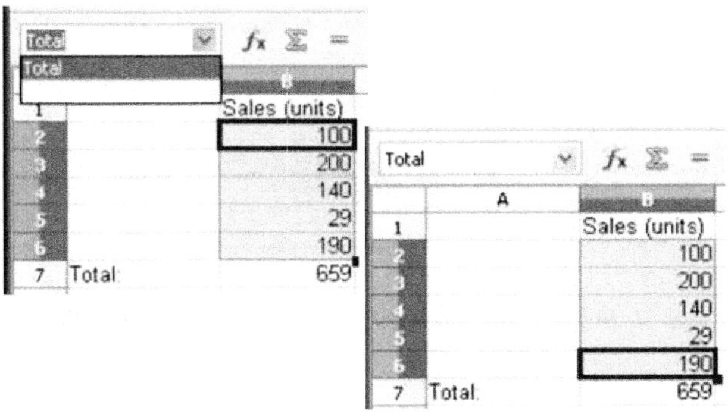

Figure 2.3: Selecting groups of named cells.

Referencing Data Stored on Other Computers

You can also refer to external documents stored on the intranet or the world-wide web. To do that, choose **Insert ⇨ Link to External Data...**

Giving Cells Names

Although addresses are a very powerful mechanism for writing formulas they are difficult to remember. Luckily, there is a way to make your life easier. OpenOffice.org Calc lets you name each cell or whole groups of cells and use those names instead of addresses. This is how you go about doing it:

1. Select the cell you want to name.
2. Choose **Insert ⇨ Names ⇨ Define**.
3. Type the cell name (such as `Total`) into the **Name** field in the **Define Names** dialog box (see Figure 2.2 on the previous page).

☞ The names must begin with a letter and should not contain spaces, and they must be unique to distinguish them from other names.

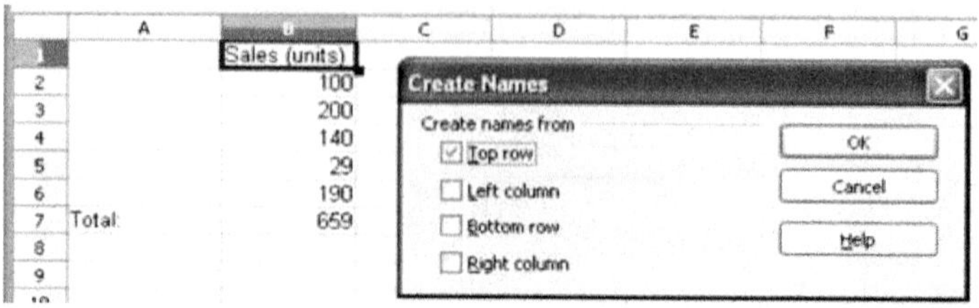

Figure 2.4: The cells you select for automatic naming must already have column or row labels.

- The **Refers to** field contains the absolute address of the cell.

4. Click on the **Add** button. That's it! You can now use the new name instead of the cell's address (for example, use =`Total` instead of =`A1`).

- You can just as easily create names for blocks of cells. Simply select as many as you like and repeat the preceding steps.

- To select any cell or a range of cells that has a defined name, select the name from the list in the top-left corner of the worksheet window. (See Figure 2.3 on the previous page.)

There is another method of creating names for blocks of cells if you already have labels above, below, to the left, or to the right of each column or row of data:

1. Select cells as in Figure 2.9 and choose **Insert ⇨ Names ⇨ Create**.
2. In the **Create Names** dialog box, click one of the options to specify the location of the labels you want to use.
3. Click **OK** to turn the labels into cell names.
4. Check if OpenOffice.org Calc did its job right by selecting one of the names from the drop-down list on the left side of the document window (see Figure 2.3 on page 17).

Chapter 3

Functions

You might have heard that functions and formulas are difficult to master. That used to be the case a long time ago, but it is not so anymore, and it is certainly not the case with OpenOffice.org Calc.

There is some jargon to explain, but its not difficult. As you will learn on the following pages, I often use phrases such as "the formula returns x" or "the function returns x," which is just a short way of saying that the formula or the function in question has a value of **x** for the given "parameters" or "arguments," as they are called by the creators of OpenOffice.org Calc.

What is the difference between a formula and a function? A formula is something you create yourself, using standard mathematical operators, numbers, text, cell addresses, or cell ranges. You can also add functions to a formula. Functions are really just prepackaged formulas that perform certain standardized jobs or calculations or even make simple decisions.

To use a function in a formula, you need to type its name followed by parentheses. For example, the following formula uses function `SQRT` to calculate the square root of 2:

```
=SQRT(2)
```

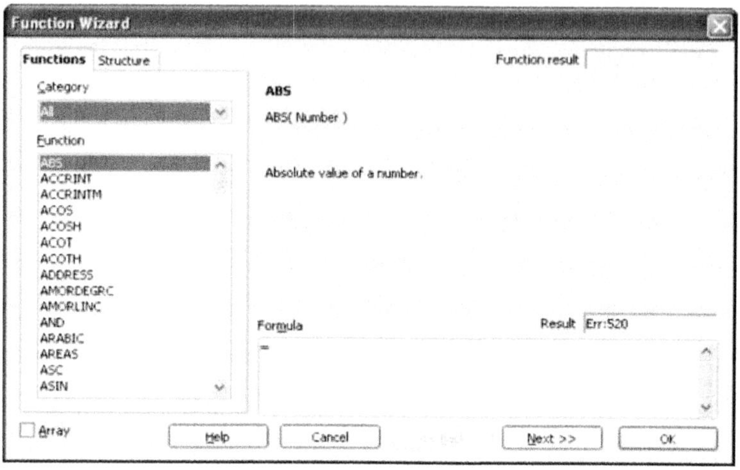

*Figure 3.1: The **Function Wizard** showing general information about functions.*

The number 2 in the formula shown on the previous page is an example of a formula *argument,* that a particular function accepts and processes to produce a result, which is then considered to be the value of the cell that the formula is held in.

- You do not have to type function names in capitals, OpenOffice.org Calc automatically corrects them for you.
- Arguments in a formula are separated by the semicolon (**;**).
- Different functions use different arguments: numbers, text, a reference to a cell that holds a number or a text string, or another function that returns a number or a piece of text.
- Using one function as an argument of another is called *nesting*. For example, you can place function PI inside function SQRT, as in

  ```
  =SQRT(PI())
  ```

  The example above shows function PI nested inside function SQRT.

*Figure 3.2: The **Function Wizard** icons.*

All functions must be followed by parentheses, even if they do not take any arguments. For example, `PI()` returns the number pi (π) and doesn't take any arguments, but still needs to be followed by parentheses.

In this book we do not put parentheses after function names to make the text easier to read and to keep in line with the conventions used by the creators of OpenOffice.org Calc. The only exception is when we include actual formula code, as in `=PI()`.

Creating Formulas by Hand

Creating formulas is as simple as typing the equal sign (=) followed by the necessary references, numbers, operators, and functions into the chosen cell and then hitting the **Enter/Return** key.

If you make mistakes in the formula, OpenOffice.org Calc complains and you can edit the formula directly inside the offending cell or on the **Input Line**. All you need to do is to place the cursor in the appropriate cell and hit **F2**.

Taming the Function Wizard

There is a better, more convenient, and less error-prone way to build formulas than by typing them into a sheet. It is called the **Function Wizard**, and it serves either as an intelligent formula editor or as a handy calculator. The wizard is shown in Figure 3.1.

Here is an exercise to help you master the **Function Wizard**:

1. Click the **Function Wizard** button on the **Spreadsheet** toolbar. (See Figure 3.2).

2. Choose a formula category, such as **Financial**, from the **Category** drop-down list on the **Functions** tab. You have the following categories to choose from:

- **Last Used** — OpenOffice.org Calc remembers which function you used recently so you don't have to hunt for them over and over again.
- **All** — a long list of all 300+ functions available in OpenOffice.org Calc.
- **Database** — database-like functions that operate on data arranged in rows. You can use them to write formulas that process large amount of data in a way similar to a database.
- **Date&Time** — functions for processing date and time values.
- **Financial** — financial functions.
- **Information** — information functions that provide additional information about formula results.
- **Logical** — basic logical functions.
- **Mathematical** — various math functions.
- **Array** — array/matrix processing functions.
- **Statistical** — statistical functions.
- **Spreadsheet** — spreadsheet information functions.
- **Text** — text processing functions.
- **Add-in** — additional statistical/programmers' functions.

3. Click the name of the function you want, such as `EFFECTIVE`. A short description of that function appears on the right-hand side panel.
4. Double-click the name of the chosen function. The right-hand side panel changes into a fill-in-the-blank form, with fields for every argument.
5. Enter function arguments into appropriate fields. Try entering `10%` into the `NOM` field and `12` into the `P` field. The **Function**

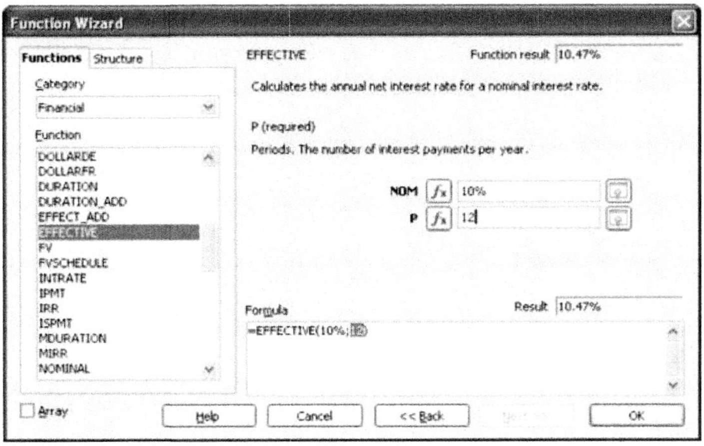

Figure 3.3: Fill-in-the-blanks forms make designing formulas much easier than doing the work by hand.

result box in the top right corner of the **Function Wizard** dialog box displays the value of that function. In the **Formula** field, you see the actual formula that OpenOffice.org Calc wrote while you were filling in the form fields. See Figure 3.3 to see how your formula should look.

6. Click **OK**.

That's it. You have created a new formula now, without worrying too much about syntax rules and matching parentheses!

The tiny **Array** option box in the bottom-left corner of the **Function Wizard** dialog box is automatically marked with a tick when the result of a function is a matrix. You do not have to turn it on or off yourself unless you want to specifically stop OpenOffice.org Calc from inserting results as a matrix.

Constructing Complex Formulas

The **Function Wizard** can be used to build some really complex formulas. Try this exercise to see what it can do. We are going to create a function that reads the current date (year, month, day), adds one to the year number, and returns the day of the week for that future date:

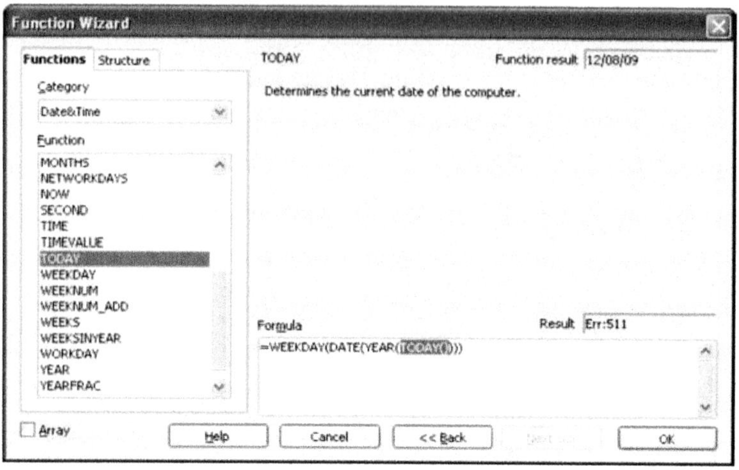

Figure 3.4: When you want to use another function as an argument, place the text cursor inside the original function's parentheses and choose the new function from the list.

1. Open the OpenOffice.org Calc **Function Wizard**.
2. Select **Date&Time** from the **Category** list.
3. Double-click the `WEEKDAY` function on the **Function** list. The right hand side panel changes into a fill-in-the-blanks form, with fields for every argument of that function.
4. Place the mouse pointer over the parentheses after the `WEEKDAY` function displayed in the **Formula** field and click. Make sure that the text cursor is inside the parentheses.
5. Choose the `DATE` function from the **Function** list on the left and double-click it.
6. Place the mouse pointer over the parentheses after the `DATE` function displayed in the **Formula** field and click. Make sure that the text cursor is inside the parentheses.
7. Choose the `YEAR` function from the list of functions on the left and double-click it.
8. Place the text cursor inside the `YEAR` function's parentheses and choose the `TODAY` function, as shown in Figure 3.4

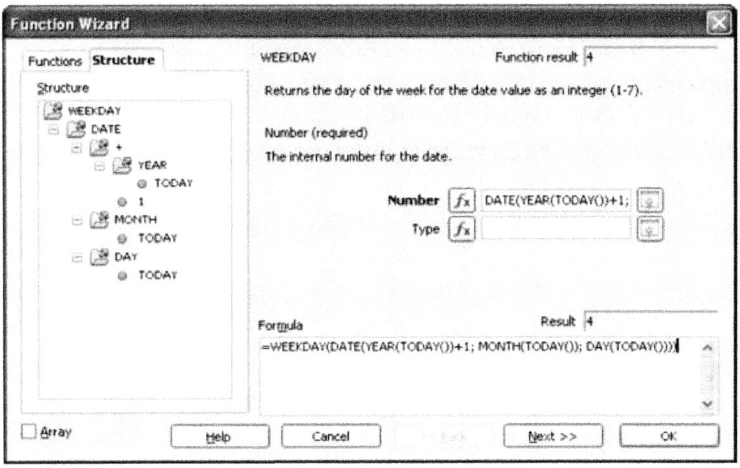

Figure 3.5: When you're lost, check the structure of the formula visually.

9. Place the text cursor after the `YEAR(TODAY())` part of the formula and type `+1`.

10. Place the text cursor after the `(YEAR(TODAY())+1)` part of the formula and type the semicolon sign (;). You have entered the first argument of a rather complex function.

11. Using the techniques described previously, create the following formula:

```
DATE((YEAR(TODAY())+1; MONTH(TODAY());
DAY(TODAY()))
```

12. The whole formula ought to look like this:

```
=WEEKDAY(DATE((YEAR(TODAY())+1; MONTH(TODAY());
DAY(TODAY())))
```

13. Click **OK**. That's it. You have created a really complex formula, and it wasn't too bad, was it?

If you get lost, you might want to use the **Structure** tab in the **Function Wizard** dialog box, which visually displays the structure of the formulas you are creating (see Figure 3.5). If there are serious errors, it shows them as red spots on the list.

You can use the **Function Wizard** to do calculations without entering them into a sheet. Just compose the formula and enter appropriate values, but do not click **OK**. The results for the whole formula are shown in the **Result** box above the **Formula** field.

Chapter 4

Formatting

OpenOffice.org Calc offers advanced data and document formatting tools. You can format sheets, cells, dates, time, numbers, text, charts, and many other objects. You can change fonts, colors, alignment, numeric formats and anything in between and beyond.

☞ The number of available tweaks can be at times overwhelming, which is why the most popular formatting actions are located on the main toolbar (see Figure 4.1 on the next page).

Formatting Text

Formatting cells and sheets in the OpenOffice.org Calc worksheets is as easy as using a word processor to prettify your CV. The layout of the documents may be different, because you store smaller pieces of information in tiny cells instead of putting it all in paragraphs on a long, blank page, but the general concepts are familiar.

When it comes to formatting, the only major difference between spreadsheets and word processors is the refined control you get over formatting numbers.

Formatting Action	Icon
Display the Styles and Formatting dialog	
Font Name list	Arial
Font Size list	10
Bold	B
Italics	I
Underline	U
Align Left	
Align Center Horizontally	
Align Right	
Justified	
Merge Cells	
Number Format: Currency	
Number Format: Percent	%
Number Format: Standard	
Number Format: Add Decimal Place	
Number Format: Delete Decimal Place	
Decrease Indent	
Increase Indent	
Borders	
Background Color	
Font Color	

Table 4.1: Popular cell formatting tools can be found on the ***Formatting*** *toolbar.*

Figure 4.1: Cell formatting tools.

The Formatting Toolbar

The most popular formatting content and document tools can be found on the **Formatting** toolbar. (see Table 4.1.). We will discuss formatting in detail in the following sections.

Cell Content Alignment

The text you enter into a cell will be treated as if it was handled by a word processor on a tiny page. That's OK, it's not like you will be using OpenOffice.org Calc to write the next *War and Peace.*

OpenOffice.org Calc will alight text to the left and numbers to the right by default. You can change text alignment using four buttons: **Align Left**, **Align Center Horizontally**, **Align Right**, **Justified** (see Table 4.1). Alternatively, you can use the following handy keyboard shortcuts:

- **Left. (Ctrl+L)** – align to the left.
- **Center. (Ctrl+E)** – center.
- **Justify. (Ctrl+J)** – justify.
- **Right. (Ctrl+R)** – align to the right.
- Content alignment tools will align all types of content, not just text and numbers.

If you want to have even more alignment options, right click on the cell you want to boss around or press **Ctrl+1** and click on the **Alignment** tab. (See Figure 4.2 on the next page.)

The tools on that tab duplicate most of the **Formatting** toolbar's functionality, but add nine additional tools that control text orientation, vertical alignment, wrapping, etc.

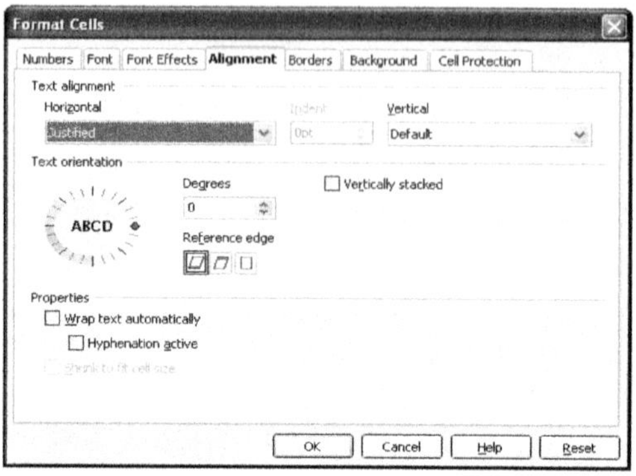

Figure 4.2: A rich set of content alignments tools can be found on the Alignment tab ***Format Cells*** *dialog.*

Here are the additional cell content adjustment options:

- **Text alignment** (Horizontal) — horizontal alignment: left, right, center, justified, filled.
- **Text alignment** (Indent) — paragraph indentation (activated when the horizontal alignment is set to left).
- **Text alignment** (Vertical) — vertical alignment (top, middle, bottom).
- **Text orientation** (Degrees) — the angle of rotation.
- **Text orientation** (Reference edge) — the reference edge for rotation.
- **Text orientation** (Vertically stacked) — text arranged vertically, but not rotated.
- **Properties** (Wrap text automatically) — turn automatic text wrap on/off. When off, the contents longer than the cell's width will not overflow the cell's edges.
- **Properties** (Hyphenation active) — turn text hyphenation on/off.

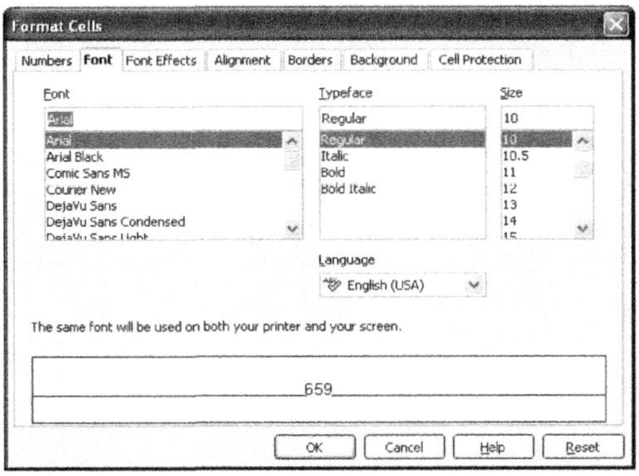

*Figure 4.3: The Font formatting options available in the **Format Cells** dialog.*

- **Properties** (Shrink to fit cell size) — activated when you use rotation.

Text Styling

Once you sort out content alignment you may want to adjust the styling of text and numbers. Just like content adjustment settings, the most popular styling options have quick access buttons on the **Formatting** toolbar. These are: **Font Name**, **Font Size**, **Bold**, **Italics**, and **Underline**. (See Table 4.1 on page 26.) They let you change fonts, font size, and switch between three common type styles.

- While using beautiful, expensive fonts to make your documents look professional no matter how bad the numbers they present, try to resist the temptation if those documents are going to be shared with others. The people you are going to share your files with are most likely not going to have a copy of *066.FONT's Crazy David No 1*

- Always use the standard Arial, Verdana, Georgia and Times fonts is the best choice for smooth portability as those fonts are available on Linux, Mac OS X, and Microsoft Windows.

If you don't like clicking on buttons, here are useful keyboard shortcuts:

- **Bold (Ctrl+B)** – switch to **bold**.
- **Italics (Ctrl+I)** – switch to *italics*.
- **Underline (Ctrl+U)** – switch to underline.
- **Remove all formatting (Ctrl+M)**.

When you can't accomplish the desired results using the tools found on the **Formatting** toolbar, use the **Format Cells** dialog box. (See Figure 4.3 on the previous page.)

The **Font** tab duplicates the text formatting functionality found on the **Formatting** toolbar and wouldn't be of much interest if it wasn't for the **Language** drop-down menu that lets you specify the language the text stored inside the selected cells is written in.

- Although it is not immediately obvious, the language setting affect the spelling procedures, which is especially beneficial for the user speaking languages that have different local 'flavors,' such as U.K. English and U.S. English as well as for those who need to create multi-language documents.
- Another cool use for the **Fonts** tab is font preview, box in the lower part of the **Format Cells** dialog.
- To dismiss the **Format Cells** dialog press **Esc** or click on the **Cancel** button.

Numeric Formats

Internally, OpenOffice.org Calc doesn't make any distinction between different kinds of numbers. No matter what numeric data you enter into your worksheet, if it looks like a number it will be stored as a number. How they appear to our eyes is decided using a set of rules called numeric formats.

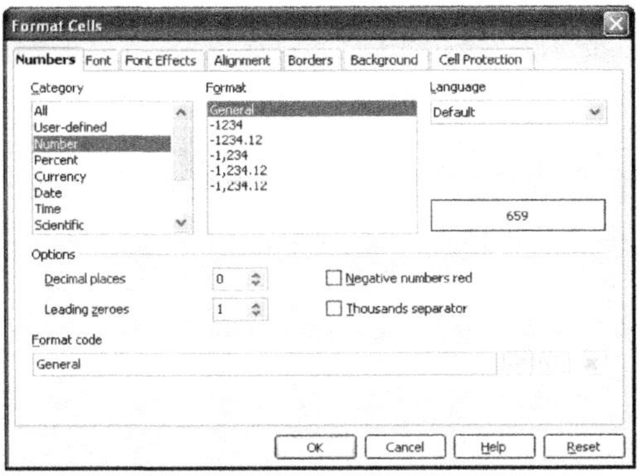

Figure 4.4: How would you like your numbers?

Quick formatting of numbers can be done when you are entering them (see page 2) or afterwards using the numeric formatting buttons on the **Formatting** toolbar. (see Table 4.1). But if you need more, there a huge list of formats available on the **Numbers** tab in the **Format Cells** dialog box (choose **Format ⇨ Cells** or right-click the selected cell or cell) and choose **Format Cells** from the pop-up menu).

OpenOffice.org Calc offers literally dozens of predefined numeric formats grouped into ten categories: **User-defined**, **Number**, **Percent**, **Currency**, **Date**, **Time**, **Scientific**, **Fraction**, **Boolean Value**, and **Text**. Simply choose the category that closely matches the kind of information you want to enter into the sheet, and click OK.

If you see a format that is almost, but not quite, the one you like, choose it and modify in the **Options** section of the **Format Cells** dialog box. Also, when you prepare documents in foreign languages, it is possible to choose the language used for text in dates (names of days, months) and time (AM, PM).

The display precision is controlled by the **Decimal places** scroll box. Internally, the numbers are processed with maximum possible precision.

Type of data	Syntax
the dollar sign	$
name of a currency	CCC
a digit	#
a thousands separator	, (comma)
decimal point or period (in dates)	. (period)
percent sign	%
ordinary fraction	?/?
exponential part	E or e
date separator	/ or -
time separator	:
color used in conditional formatting	[name]
day number (without leading zeros)	D
day number (with leading zeros)	DD
short name of a day	DDD or NNN
full name of a day	DDDD
full name of a day followed by a comma	NNNN
month number (without leading zeroes)	M
month number (with leading zeroes)	MM
short name of a month	MMM
full name of a month	MMMM
a two-digit year number	YY
a four-digit year number	YYYY
the short name of a calendar quarter	Q
the name of a calendar quarter	QQ
a two-digit week number	WW

Figure 4.2: The Conditional Formatting dialog box in all its glory.

☞ The numeric formats are independent of the text styles applied to them. Any cell can be assigned any combination of numeric formats and text styles (font, alignment, etc.).

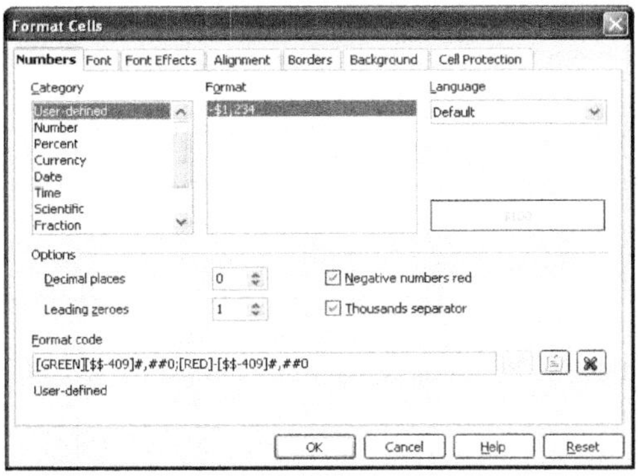

Figure 4.5: Your first custom numeric format.

Creating Your Own Numeric Formats

Not enough numeric formats? Create your own! It is easy, although by no means as intuitive as other activities in OpenOffice.org Calc.

The best strategy is to start with the format that closely resembles the one you are trying to create and then modify it in the **Format code** input box. For example, you might like to create a format that displays money in green (when greater than zero) or red (when less than zero). Here is how you go about doing it:

1. Place the spreadsheet cursor in the chosen cell.

2. Choose **Format ⇨ Cells**.

3. In the **Format Cells** dialog box, choose category **Currency**.

4. Choose format `-$1,234.00` (shown in red).

5. Click the format code at the bottom of the dialog box and add `[GREEN]` at the beginning.

6. Click the green check mark button to add your new style (it will be listed in the **User-defined** category) and the yellow comment button to add comments, which are then displayed under the **Format** code box in the **Numbers** tab. When you look closely at the various formats' codes, you notice that they use some special commands. Table 4.2 explains what they do.

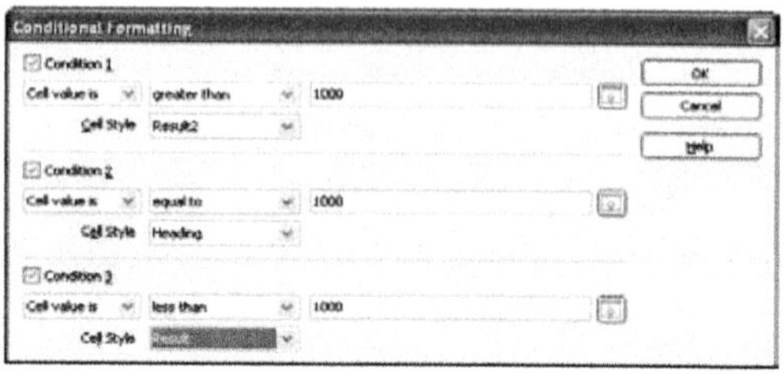

Figure 4.6: Setting up conditional formatting.

Creating Conditional Formatting

Conditional formatting is one of those brilliant ideas that make your work a little bit easier and more fun. Conditional formatting is a great help if you want to test several choices. For example, if you are a salesperson or a manager, you might want to test several scenarios during negotiations.

It is not always to your advantage to reveal exact numbers, and this is when conditional formatting can help. It changes the style of one or more cells according to the preset conditions, which remain unseen to other people. Having visual cues is a great thing during negotiations, you know it is OK to give the discount the client asks for when you see black or green and you know that the client is asking for impossible when you see red.

- Each cell can have up to three conditions, based on the value stored inside the cell or the value of a formula stored inside that cell, or the value of another cell that the current cell refers to.

- To set these conditions, choose **Format ➪ Conditional Formatting** and enter the numbers into the condition boxes, as shown in Figure 4.6. After you do that, choose a different style for each condition and click **OK**. Next, type several numbers that belong to the ranges you just defined into that cell and see them displayed in different styles.

The default cell styles are not very useful, therefore you need to create them, one at a time, and import them into the **Styles and**

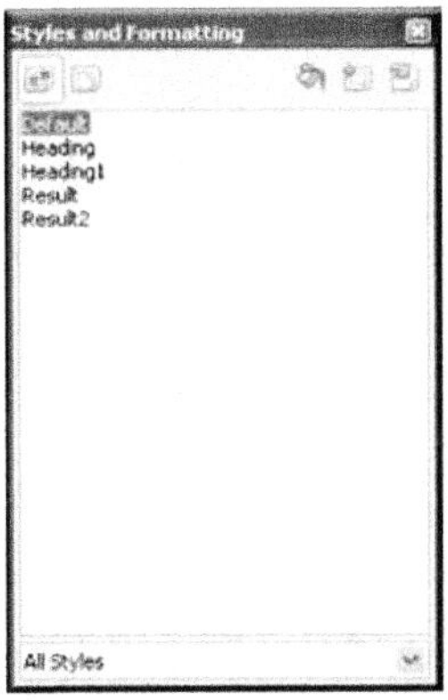

Figure 4.7: The ***Styles and Formatting*** *manager.*

Formatting manager (press **F11**). After that, they are available in the **Conditional Formatting** dialog box.

The easiest way to go about creating styles is just following the advice presented in the previous sections of this chapter and experimenting until you are happy with your data's looks. Then, simply select the cell whose style you'd like to preserve, press F11, and click on the **New Style from Selection** button (it has a tiny green plus sign) and give it a name.

Even more advanced conditional formatting can be achieved through the use of the OpenOffice.org Calc's built-in functions, such as STYLE, which can change the style of a cell or a range of cells according to certain conditions set by the user.

Formatting Cells

Formatting cells (not the contents stored inside them) is done almost purely to emphasize certain facts presented on a sheet. From the designer's point of view, a cell consists of the following elements:

- **Background color.** This can be set with the **Background** button on the **Formatting** toolbar or by choosing **Format ⇨ Cell**, clicking the **Background** tab in the **Format Cells** dialog box, and selecting the right color.
- **Borders.** These have their own tab (**Borders**, of course) in the **Format Cells** dialog box and can be set to any color from the available list. Also, you can add shadows when you want to make something really stand out of the crowd.

Formatting Columns and Rows

Formatting columns and rows is limited to changing their width or height, hiding or showing them, and automatically choosing their optimal width or height. All of these can be performed using the **Format ⇨ Column** or **Format ⇨ Row** submenu.

- You can also change width and height by placing the mouse pointer between the buttons with column (or row) numbers and dragging the boundary lines until they look the way you want them to.
- Even better, OpenOffice.org Calc can automatically adjust column width and row height, just place the mouse pointer between the separator buttons and double-click.

Formatting Worksheets

Formatting a worksheet is the top-most level of document design, here you create the final layout of your work on paper. Here you can specify the size of paper used for printing, headers, footers, page numbers, and so on.

- You can't design separate layouts for individual sheets, but that is not a big problem, because you can use separate worksheets if you need different layouts.

The main page layout options are available in the **Page Style** dialog box pictured in Figure 4.8.

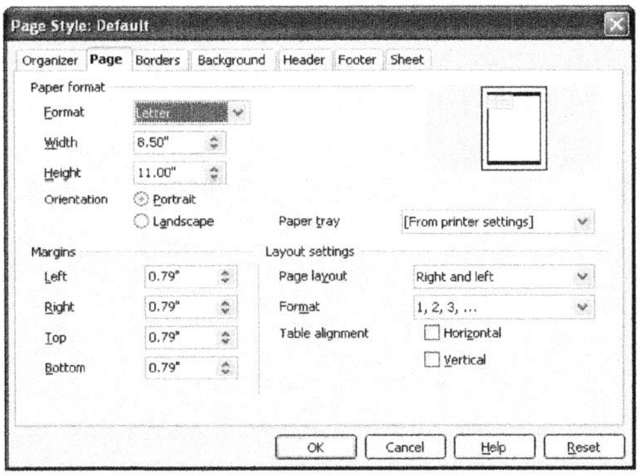

Figure 4.8: The ***Page Style*** *dialog box manages the final look of the printed pages.*

Choose **Format ⇨ Page** to display the **Page Style** dialog box. There are seven tabs in this dialog box:

- **Organizer**. Enables you to choose one of the page styles available for this sheet.

- **Page**. You can set **Margins** (useful when your printer seems to chop off parts of the printout), **Paper Format** (paper size, page orientation, and paper source), which you need to specify to make your printer use the right paper, if you have more than one source; otherwise use **Printer** settings, and **Orientation**, which should really be called **Alignment** of cells on paper—click the options and see the preview box to check the results.

- **Borders**. Here you can set the borders for the page.

- **Background**. Similar to formatting cells, you can set the page background color. It is advisable that you do not use any color for printing (**No fill**) even if you have a color printer, because it is very expensive to print pages with color background. Use it only if you are printing final versions of promotional materials, and money is no object.

- **Header**. Here you can specify what, if anything, is to be printed at the top of each page. Also, headers can have their own borders and background, click **More** to edit these properties. If you want to edit the content of the header itself, click **Edit**. You can have separate headers for left and right pages, if you print on both sides of paper. To use them, deselect the **Same content left/right** option.

- **Footer**. Everything that applies to headers also applies to footers.
- **Sheet**. Default values on this sheet can be left alone, unless you want to print cell notes, grid, formulas, or column and row headers (`A … IV` and `1 … 32,000`) which is not necessary in most cases. However, you might change the **Page order**, if the pages progress from left to right instead of top to bottom, and, if necessary, you can specify the maximum number of pages that may be used in printing and let OpenOffice.org Calc scale them down accordingly. Do not expect miracles, but you might be able to save one page for each 6 to 10 pages. It depends on the size of the sheet and the resolution of your printer (600 dpi is best).

Sometimes OpenOffice.org Calc breaks pages in places where you would rather they were not broken. To remedy that, place the cursor in a cell where you want to insert a page break and choose **Insert ➪ Manual Break ➪ Row Break** or **Insert ➪ Manual Break ➪ Column Break** to insert the page break either above or to the left of the cell.

Removing manual breaks is just as easy, choose **Edit ➪ Remove Manual Break ➪ Row Break** or **Edit ➪ Remove Manual Break ➪ Column Break**.

Autoformatting Sheets

If you would like to avoid the tedious formatting of cells by hand, use pre-defined formats:

1. Enter data into a sheet in some roughly organized manner.
2. Choose **Format ➪ AutoFormat**.

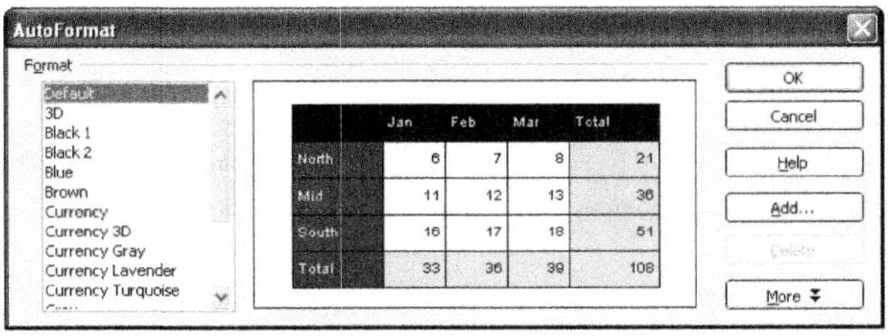

Figure 4.9: Autoformat.

3. Select the format you like from the list on the left. (See Figure 4.9.)

4. Click on the **OK** button. You're done.

Adding New Designs to the Autoformat List

You can create your own sheet designs and add them to the list of format in the **Autoformat** dialog:

1. Enter data into a sheet in some roughly organized manner.
2. Select the formatted area.
3. Choose **Format ⇨ AutoFormat**.
4. Click the **Add...** button in the **Autoformat** dialog box.
5. Type in the name of your new format.
6. Click on the **OK** button. That's it!

☞ Your new format must be at least 4 cells by 4 cells in size to be accepted by OpenOffice.org Calc.

Chapter 5

Simple Mathematical Functions

In this chapter you are going to learn about popular OpenOffice.org Calc mathematical functions. It is a good idea to try the examples from this chapter to see how OpenOffice.org Calc work.

Absolute Values of Numbers (ABS)

Syntax: ABS(n)

The `ABS` function removes the minus sign (-) from a negative number, making it positive. It does nothing to `0` (zero) or positive numbers.

	A	B	C
10	ABS	Number	Result
11	ABS	-2	2
12	ABS	0	0
13	ABS	2	2

*Figure 5.1: Sample results of the **ABS** function.*

The **ABS** function is useful, if you want to further process values returned by a formula or function that may return negative results. For example:

```
=SQRT(PMT(7.5%/12; 25*12; 1,000,000))
```

produces errors, because the `PMT` function (see "Calculations with Money" later in this book on page 71) returns negative values for payments due. It is mathematically correct, but may be confusing to some. To change that result to a positive number, use

```
=SQRT(ABS(PMT(7.5%/12; 25*12; 1,000,000)))
```

By the way, if you want to add the minus sign on every result, use

```
=-SQRT(ABS(PMT(7.5%/12; 25*12; 1,000,000)))
```

☞ **Remember**. When you start wrapping functions and formulas in `ABS`, you alter their results in a way that may not be expected by other functions and formulas that rely on those results. Always think twice about the consequences of such modifications.

☞ See also the section on the `SIGN` function.

Exponential Function (EXP)

Syntax: EXP(number)

Returns the values of the exponential function e^x for the given number x; where e is approximately equal to `2.718281828`. For example:

	A	B	C
15	EXP	Number	Result
16	EXP	1	2.72

*Figure 5.2: Sample result of the **EXP** function.*

```
=EXP(1)
```

returns 2.72. (See Figure 5.2.)

See also the sections on the FACT (page 43), LN (page 44), LOG (page 44), LOG10 (page 45), POWER (page 46), and SQRT (page 47) functions.

	A	B	C
18	FACT	Number	Result
19	FACT	3	6

*Figure 5.3: Sample result of the **FACT** function.*

Factorial Function (FACT)

Syntax: FACT(n)

The FACT function returns the value of the factorial function for the given number (the product of all integers from 1 to n). For example:

```
=FACT(3)
```

returns 6 or 1 * 2 * 3.

See also the section on the EXP function on page 42.

	A	B	C
21	LN	Number	Result
22	LN	8	2.08

*Figure 5.4: Sample result of the **LN** functions.*

Natural Logarithm (LN)

Syntax: LN(number)

The `LN` function returns the value of the natural logarithm (the logarithm base of *e*) for the given `number`. For example:

```
=LN(8)
```

returns 2.08 ($\log_e 8$).

> See also the sections on the `EXP` (page 42), `LOG` (page 44), `LOG10` (page 45), and `POWER` (page 46) functions.

	A	B	C	D
24	LOG	Number	Base	Result
25	LOG	8	2.08	2.84

*Figure 5.5: Sample result of the **LOG** functions.*

Logarithm (LOG)

Syntax: LOG(number; base)

The `LOG` function returns the value of the user-defined-base logarithm for the given `number`. For example:

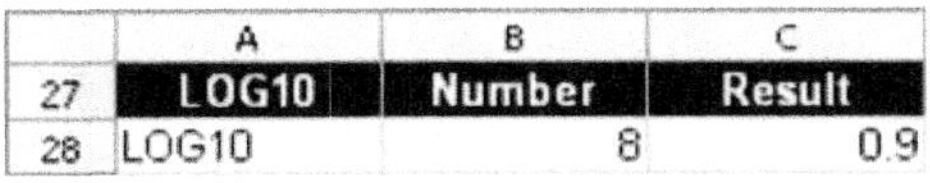

Figure 5.6: Sample result of the ***LOG10*** *functions.*

=LOG(8; 4)

returns 1.5 ($\log_8 4$).

See also the sections on the EXP (page 42), LN (page 44), LOG10 (page 45), and POWER (page 46) functions.

Logarithm Base 10 (LOG10)

Syntax: LOG10(number)

The LOG10 function returns the value of logarithm base 10 for the given number. For example:

=LOG10(8)

is 0.9 ($\log_{10} 8$).

See also the sections on the EXP (page 42), LN (page 44), LOG (page 44), and POWER (page 46) functions.

	A	B	C	D
30	POWER	Number	Power	Result
31	POWER	10	2	100

Figure 5.7: Sample result of the ***POWER*** *function.*

Power (POWER)

Syntax: POWER(number; power)

The POWER functions returns number raised to the given power. For example:

```
=POWER(10; 2)
```

returns 100, or 10^2. It is equivalent to the following notation:

```
=10^2
```

See also the sections on the EXP (page 42), FACT (page 43), LN (page 44), LOG (page 44), LOG10 (page 45), and SQRT functions.

Product of Many Arguments (PRODUCT)

Syntax: PRODUCT(ARG1; ARG2; . . . ARG30)

The PRODUCT function multiplies up to 30 arguments (x1, x2, ... x30). Each argument can be a single value or a range of cells. For example:

```
=PRODUCT(A1:A23; B2:C23)
```

	A	B	C	D
33	PRODUCT	ARG1	ARG2	ARG3
34	PRODUCT	10	2	100
35		ARG4	ARG5	ARG6
36		10	2	100
37	Result	ARG7	ARG8	ARG9
38	8000000000	10	2	100

Figure 5.8: Sample result of the ***PRODUCT*** *function.*

multiplies values of all cells from ranges `A1:A23` and `B2:C23`.

☞ See also the section on the `SUM` function on page 48.

	A	B	C
40	SQRT	Number	Result
41	SQRT	10	3.16

Figure 5.9: Sample result of the ***SQRT*** *function.*

Square Root (SQRT)

Syntax: SQRT(number)

The `SQRT` function returns the square root of a positive `number`. For example, to find a square root of `10`, you'd type:

```
=SQRT(10)
```

The answer is, of course, `3.16`.

When you need to calculate the square root of a negative value, use the `ABS` function to remove the negative sign (see the description of the `ABS` function earlier in this section on page 41).

	A	B	C	D
43	SUM	ARG1	ARG2	ARG3
44	SUM	10	2	100
45		ARG4	ARG5	ARG6
46		10	2	100
47	Result	ARG7	ARG8	ARG9
48	336	10	2	100

Figure 5.10: Sample result of the ***SUM*** *function.*

- Strictly speaking, this is not correct from a mathematical point of view, because you cannot computer a square root of a negative number, but it is perfectly acceptable when you deal with the results produced by financial functions. If you are using a method that specifically forbids this trick, you need to work with complex numbers.

- OpenOffice.org Calc does provide functions for dealing with complex numbers, if you need to obey the laws of mathematics. A proper discussion of complex numbers is outside of the scope of this book, by any decent college math textbook will help you understand them.

- Also see the section on the POWER function on page 46.

Sum of Many Arguments (SUM)

Syntax: SUM(x1; x2; .... x30)

The SUM function adds up to 30 arguments x1,x2, ... x3 and each such argument can be a range of cells. For example:

```
=PRODUCT(M1:N23; Z2:AA23)
```

adds all cells from ranges M1:N23 and Z2:AA23.

- See also the section on the PRODUCT function on page 46.

	A	B	C	D
50	SUMSQ	ARG1	ARG2	ARG3
51	SUMSQ	10	2	100
52		ARG4	ARG5	ARG6
53		10	2	100
54	Result	ARG7	ARG8	ARG9
55	30312	10	2	100

Figure 5.11: Sample result of the ***SUMSQ*** *function.*

Sum of Squares of Many Arguments (SUMSQ)

Syntax: SUMSQ(x1; x2; ... x30)

The SUMSQ function adds squares of up to 30 arguments x1, x2, ... x30 and each such argument can be a range of cells. For example:

```
=SUMSQ(M1:N23; Z2:AA23)
```

adds all squares of the numeric values held in cells from ranges M1:N23 and Z2:AA23.

See also the section on the SUM function on page 48.

Chapter 6

Utility Mathematical Functions

In this chapter you will get to know useful functions that help you solve many practical problems related to crunching numbers.

Nearest Multiple Larger Than or Equal To X (CEILING)

Syntax: CEILING(number; significance; mode)

The `CEILING` function rounds the given `number` up to the nearest multiple of `significance` equal to or greater than `number` itself. It is used in filtering noise out of a large number of values, spotting

	A	B	C	D	E
57	CEILING	Number	Significance	Mode	Result
58	CEILING	-13	-4	1	-16
59	CEILING	-13	-4	0	-12
60	CEILING	-13	-4		-12

Figure 6.1: Sample results of the ***CEILING*** *function.*

significant changes in values, detecting trend reversals, and similar tasks where it is easier to work with multiples of integers to get a better understanding of the sea of data you need to work with.

The `CEILING` function is also a great tool for solving mundane problems like ordering the right amount of boxes for shipping. For example, suppose you have `125,000` unsold USB drives that you want to get rid of using that old "buy-thirteen-get-five-free" technique. Why thirteen and five? Because the cheapest boxes you could find will hold a maximum of `18` drives and you want to sound original. Here's how you use `CEILING`:

```
=CEILING(125,000; 18)
```

The result you will get is 125,010. This tells you how many USB sticks you would need to fill all boxes with exactly `18` USB drives. But you only have `125,000` USB drives. That's OK. One of the boxes will have less than `18` USB drives. You will give a special discount on those or just give them away. But you still don't know how many boxes you'll need. Here's how to get that number:

```
=CEILING(125,000; 18)/18
```

And the answer is `6945`.

What if those boxes are sold one dozen per package? How many packages should you order?

```
=CEILING(CEILING(125,000; 18)/18; 12)/12
```

And here is the answer: `579` packages.

> Upon close inspection, you could say that `CEILING` is similar to `ROUND` or `ROUNDUP`, but it is only partially true. While the `ROUND` function will obey the math rules for rounding fractional numbers and round them up and down accordingly, `CEILING` always rounds up. The `ROUNDUP`

	A	B	C
62	EVEN	Number	Result
63	EVEN	13	14

Figure 6.2: Sample result of the ***EVEN*** *function.*

function is closer in its behavior to CEILING, but needs a little more typing, e.g. you have to specify the number of decimal places for results.

The third argument in CEILING, mode, is used to specify rounding rules for negative numbers. When you omit this argument, the number is rounded up to the nearest multiple of a given negative number. For example:

```
=CEILING(-13; -2)
```

returns -12, which is greater than -13, unless you add 1 as mode, as in

```
=CEILING(-13; -2; 1)
```

which returns -14.

You cannot mix negative and positive numbers. For example: CEILING(-13;2) is not allowed.

See also the sections on the EVEN (page 53), FLOOR (page 54), INT (page 55), ODD (page 56), ROUND (page 57), ROUNDDOWN (page 58), ROUNDUP (page 59), and TRUNC (page 59) functions.

Nearest Even Integer (EVEN)

Syntax: EVEN(number)

The EVEN function is useful when you want results to be presented as even integer numbers. It rounds the given number up to the nearest even integer, which is just what you need if you need to

	A	B	C	D	E
65	FLOOR	Number	Significance	Mode	Result
66	FLOOR	-13	-4	1	-12
67	FLOOR	-13	-4	0	-16
68	FLOOR	-13	-4		-16

*Figure 6.3: Sample results of the **FLOOR** function.*

count quantities such as "pairs of socks" or "pairs of gloves" (but not "pairs of trousers"). For example: if your worksheet reports that you need to sell 12,467.349888 socks to pay off the money gods, use the following formula to turn that cold number into something a human can understand:

```
=EVEN(12,467.349888)/2
```

The result will be 6234 pairs of socks, which is a much more useful and natural way to present such quantities. Of course, you do not have to put the actual number into that function; a reference to another cell that store the value to be rounded up is as useful, as is nesting of another function inside the EVEN function.

See also the sections on the CEILING (page 51), INT (page 55), FLOOR (page 54), ODD (page 56), ROUND (page 57), ROUNDDOWN (page 58), and ROUNDUP (page 59) functions.

Nearest Multiple Smaller or Equal to X (FLOOR)

Syntax: FLOOR(number; significance; mode)

The FLOOR function rounds the given number down to the nearest multiple of significance. It is similar to CEILING, but instead of "padding" the given numbers, it will "shave a little off their top". For example, in the section on the CEILING functions presented earlier in this chapter you read about looking for the number of boxes needed to pack 18 USB drives given the total number of those drives and the fact that the boxes are sold in dozens. As you recall,

	A	B	C
70	INT	Number	Result
71	INT	12.6	12

*Figure 6.4: Sample result of the **INT** function.*

one box will have less than 18 drives in it. You can use the FLOOR function to find out how many boxes you would need to buy if you wanted to have exactly 18 drives in each and keep the remainder unboxed. Here's the formula you need:

```
=FLOOR(125,000; 18)/18
```

And the answer is 6944.

Negative values are rounded down to the nearest multiple of a given negative number. For example:

```
=FLOOR(-13; -2)
```

returns `-14`, unless you add `1` as `mode`, as in

```
=FLOOR(-13; -2; 1)
```

which returns `-12`.

You cannot mix negative and positive numbers. For example, `FLOOR(-13;2)` is not allowed.

See also the sections on the CEILING (page 51), EVEN (page 53), INT (page 55), ODD (page 56), ROUND (page 57), ROUNDDOWN (page 58), ROUNDUP (page 59), and TRUNC (page 59) functions.

Nearest Integer (INT)

Syntax: INT(number)

The `INT` function rounds the given `number` down to the nearest integer. For example:

	A	B	C
73	**ODD**	**Number**	**Result**
74	ODD	12.6	13

Figure 6.5: Sample result of the ***ODD*** *function.*

=INT(12.3)

returns 12.

See also the sections on the CEILING (page 51), EVEN (page 53), FLOOR (page 54), ODD (page 56), ROUND (page 57), ROUNDDOWN (page 58), and ROUNDUP (page 59) functions.

Nearest Odd Integer (ODD)

Syntax: ODD(number)

This is the function to use if you want results to be rounded up to the nearest odd integer. For example:

=ODD(12.3)

returns 13.

See also the sections on the CEILING (page 51), EVEN (page 53), INT (page 55), FLOOR (page 54), ROUND (page 57), ROUNDDOWN (page 58), and ROUNDUP (page 59) functions.

Random Number (RAND)

Syntax: RAND()

The RAND function returns a random fractional number between 0 and 1. To make it a bit more useful, you can multiply it by 10 and

	A	B
76	RAND	Result
77	RAND	0.65

Figure 6.6: Sample result of the ***RAND*** *function.*

use TRUNC to turn the results into integers from 0 to 10. Here's an example:

```
=TRUNC(RAND()*10)
```

Multiplying RAND by 100 in the preceding example returns numbers from 0 to 100.

If you want random numbers from a different range, such as 1,000 to 2,000, use the following trick:

```
=TRUNC(RAND()*1000)+1000
```

See also the section on the TRUNC function on page 59.

	A	B	C	D
79	ROUND	Number	Count	Result
80	ROUND	12.6543210	3	12.6540000

Figure 6.7: Sample result of the ***ROUND*** *function.*

Rounding Numbers (ROUND)

Syntax: ROUND(x; y)

The ROUND function rounds x to y decimal places, as in

```
=ROUND(1.2533; 1)
```

which returns the argument rounded to one decimal place, or 1.3.

	A	B	C	D
82	**ROUNDDOWN**	**Number**	**Count**	**Result**
83	ROUNDDOWN	12.6543210	3	12.6540000

Figure 6.8: Sample result of the ***ROUNDDOWN*** *function.*

- Using 0 as the number of decimal places rounds numbers to whole integers.

- See also the sections on the CEILING (page 51), EVEN (page 53), FLOOR (page 54), INT (page 55), ODD (page 56), and TRUNC (page 59) functions.

Rounding Numbers Down (ROUNDDOWN)

Syntax: ROUNDDOWN(x; y)

The ROUNDDOWN function does exactly what you'd expect; it rounds the first argument down to the specified number of decimal places, as in

```
=ROUNDDOWN(1.2533; 1)
```

which returns 1.2.

- Using 0 as the number of decimal places rounds numbers to whole integers.

- See also the sections on the CEILING (page 51), EVEN (page 53), FLOOR (page 54), INT (page 55), ODD (page 56), and TRUNC (page 59) functions.

	A	B	C	D
85	ROUNDUP	Number	Count	Result
86	ROUNDUP	12.6543210	3	12.6550000

*Figure 6.9: Sample result of the **ROUNDUP** function.*

Rounding Numbers Up (ROUNDUP)

Syntax: ROUNDUP(x; y)

The ROUNDUP function, just as you'd expect, rounds numeric values up to the specified number of decimal places, as in

```
=ROUNDUP(7.111; 1)
```

which returns 7.2.

Using 0 as the number of decimal places rounds numbers to whole integers.

See also the sections on the CEILING (page 51), EVEN (page 53), FLOOR (page 54), INT (page 55), ODD (page 56), and TRUNC (page 59) functions.

	A	B	C	D
88	TRUNC	Number	Count	Result
89	TRUNC	12.6543210	3	12.6540000
90	TRUNC	12.6543210		12.0000000

*Figure 6.10: Sample results of the **TRUNC** function.*

Truncate (TRUNC)

Syntax: TRUNC(x; y)

The TRUNC function is different from other rounding functions. It does not round number x, but chops off its fractional part, leaving y digits after the decimal point (if the second argument is omitted, TRUNC chops off the whole fractional part of a number turning it into an integer). For example:

```
=TRUNC(12.5)
```

returns 12. The subtle difference between TRUNC and INT is best explained when you use the same negative number as an argument for these functions, for example:

```
=TRUNC(-15.72)
```

returns -15, while

```
=INT(-15.72)
```

returns -16.

In this example TRUNC is used with a second argument and

```
=TRUNC(16.2371; 2)
```

returns 16.23.

See also the sections on the CEILING (page 51), EVEN (page 53), FLOOR (page 54), INT (page 55), ODD (page 56), ROUND (page 57), ROUNDDOWN (page 58), and ROUNDUP (page 59) functions.

For more mathematical functions click the **Function Wizard** button and choose **Mathematical** or **Matrix** from the **Categories** list.

Chapter 7

Useful Statistical Functions

Statistical functions operate on series or ranges of values. The examples in this chapter are simplified, but adequate for most purposes.

Average (AVERAGE)

Syntax: AVERAGE(x1; x2; ... x30)

The AVERAGE function returns the average of up to 30 given arguments separated with the semicolon sign (;). Each such argument may be a range of cells. For example:

	A	B	C	D
92	AVERAGE	ARG1	ARG2	ARG3
93	AVERAGE	12.55	10.93	11.78
94		ARG4	ARG5	ARG6
95		12	11.54	12.67
96	Result	ARG7	ARG8	ARG9
97	15.66	23.56	45.21	0.67

*Figure 7.1: Sample result of the **AVERAGE** function.*

```
=AVERAGE(12.55; 10.93; 11.78; 12.00; 11.54; 12.67;
23.56; 45.21; 0.67)
```

returns `15.66`.

	A	B	C	D
92	GEOMEAN	ARG1	ARG2	ARG3
93	GEOMEAN	12.55	10.93	11.78
94		ARG4	ARG5	ARG6
95		12	11.54	12.67
96	Result	ARG7	ARG8	ARG9
97	10.81	23.56	45.21	0.67

*Figure 7.2: Sample result of the **GEOMEAN** function.*

Geometric Mean (GEOMEAN)

Syntax: GEOMEAN(x1; x2; ... x30)

The `GEOMEAN` function returns the geometric mean of up to 30 given arguments separated with the semicolon sign (;). Each such argument may be a range of cells. For example:

```
=GEOMEAN(12.55; 10.93; 11.78; 12.00; 11.54; 12.67;
23.56; 45.21; 0.67)
```

returns `10.81`.

	A	B	C	D
99	HARMEAN	ARG1	ARG2	ARG3
100	HARMEAN	12.55	10.93	11.78
101		ARG4	ARG5	ARG6
102		12	11.54	12.67
103	Result	ARG7	ARG8	ARG9
104	4.36	23.56	45.21	0.67

*Figure 7.3: Sample result of the **HARMEAN** function.*

Harmonic Mean (HARMEAN)

Syntax: HARMEAN(x1; x2; ... x30)

The `HARMEAN` function returns the harmonic mean of up to 30 given arguments separated with the semicolon sign (`;`). Each such argument may be a range of cells. For example:

```
=HARMEAN(12.55; 10.93; 11.78; 12.00; 11.54; 12.67;
23.56; 45.21; 0.67)
```

returns `4.36`.

	A	B	C	D
106	MEDIAN	ARG1	ARG2	ARG3
107	MEDIAN	12.55	10.93	11.78
108		ARG4	ARG5	ARG6
109		12	11.54	12.67
110	Result	ARG7	ARG8	ARG9
111	12	23.56	45.21	0.67

*Figure 7.4: Sample result of the **MEDIAN** function.*

Median (MEDIAN)

Syntax: MEDIAN(x1; x2; ... x30)

The `MEDIAN` function returns the median of up to 30 given arguments separated with the semicolon sign (`;`). Each such

	A	B	C	D
113	COUNT	ARG1	ARG2	ARG3
114	COUNT	12.55	10.93	c
115		ARG4	ARG5	ARG6
116		12	b	12.67
117	Result	ARG7	ARG8	ARG9
118	6	a	45.21	0.67

Figure 7.5: Sample result of the ***COUNT*** *function.*

argument may be a range of cells. For example, the following function

```
=MEDIAN(12.55; 10.93; 11.78; 12.00; 11.54; 12.67;
23.56; 45.21; 0.67)
```

returns 12.

Counting Cells (COUNT)

Syntax: COUNT(x1; x2; ... x30)

The `COUNT` function accepts a maximum of 30 separate arguments (single values and ranges of cells) and returns the number of arguments that contain numeric values.

For example:

```
=COUNT("OpenOffice.org"; 7139; 12.99)
```

returns 2.

	A	B	C	D
120	COUNTA	ARG1	ARG2	ARG3
121	COUNTA	12.55	10.93	c
122		ARG4	ARG5	ARG6
123		12	b	12.67
124	Result	ARG7	ARG8	ARG9
125	9	a	45.21	0.67

Figure 7.6: Sample result of the ***COUNTA*** *function.*

Counting Cells (COUNTA)

Syntax: COUNTA(x1; x2; ... x30)

The COUNTA function accepts a maximum of 30 separate arguments, (single values and ranges of cells) and returns the number of arguments that contain any kind of values (empty cells are ignored). For example:

```
=COUNTA("OpenOffice.org"; 7139; 12.99)
```

returns 3.

	A	B	C	D
127	LARGE	ARG1	ARG2	ARG3
128	LARGE	12.55	10.93	11.78
129			Rank	Result
130			2	11.78

Figure 7.7: Sample result of the ***LARGE*** *function.*

The Kth Largest Value (LARGE)

Syntax: LARGE(x; k)

The LARGE function returns the *k*th largest numeric value found in the given set of values x. E.g., when given the set of values of 12.55,

	A	B	C	D
132	SMALL	ARG1	ARG2	ARG3
133	SMALL	12.55	10.93	11.78
134			Rank	Result
135			3	12.55

*Figure 7.8: Sample result of the **SMALL** function.*

10.93, and 11.78, LARGE returns the following result:

=LARGE(B132:D132; 3)

returns 12.55, which is the 3rd largest value in the given set.

- You can set the k argument to any integer value you like, but it must not be zero or larger than the number of elements in the given set of numbers.
- See also the sections on the SMALL (page 66), MAX (page 67), and MIN (page 67) functions.

The Kth Smallest Value (SMALL)

Syntax: SMALL(x; k)

The SMALL function returns the *k*th largest numeric value found in the given set of values **x**. E.g., when given the set of values of 12.55, 10.93, and 11.78, SMALL returns the following result:

=SMALL(B132:D132; 3)

returns 12.55. which is the 3rd smallest value in the given set.

- You can set the k argument to any integer value you like, but it must not be zero or larger than the number of elements in the given set of numbers.
- See also the sections on the LARGE (page 65), MAX (page 67) and MIN (page 67) functions.

	A	B	C	D
137	MAX	ARG1	ARG2	ARG3
138	MAX	67	2	100
139		ARG4	ARG5	ARG6
140		10	23	97
141	Result	ARG7	ARG8	ARG9
142	100	32	56	99

*Figure 7.9: Sample result of the **MAX** function.*

Maximum (MAX)

Syntax: MAX(x1; x2; ... x30)

The `MAX` function can take up to 30 arguments, which can be ranges of cells, and returns the maximum value found in the given set. For example:

```
=MAX(B138; C138; D138; B140; C140; D140, B142; C142; D142)
```

The result is 100.

See also the sections on the `LARGE` (page 65), `MIN` (page 67), and `SMALL` (page 66) functions.

	A	B	C	D
144	MIN	ARG1	ARG2	ARG3
145	MIN	67	2	100
146		ARG4	ARG5	ARG6
147		10	23	97
148	Result	ARG7	ARG8	ARG9
149	2	32	56	99

*Figure 7.10: Sample result of the **MIN** function.*

Minimum (MIN)

Syntax: MIN(x1; x2; ... x30)

The `MAX` function can take up to 30 arguments, which can be ranges of cells, and returns the maximum value found in the given set. E.g.:

	A	B	C	D
151	MODE	ARG1	ARG2	ARG3
152	MODE	67	2	100
153		ARG4	ARG5	ARG6
154		10	2	97
155	Result	ARG7	ARG8	ARG9
156	2	32	56	99

Figure 7.11: Sample result of the ***MODE*** *function.*

`=MAX(B138; C138; D138; B140; C140; D140, B142; C142; D142)`

would return 2.

See also the sections on the LARGE (page 65), MAX (page 67), and SMALL (page 66) functions.

Mode Function (MODE)

Syntax: MODE(x1; x2; ... x30)

Th MODE function returns the most common value in a data set which can consist of up to thirty arguments, which can be single values or ranges of cells. You can provide up to 30 arguments. For example, if you give MODE the following set:

67, 2, 2.10, 2, 97, 32, 56, 99

then MODE would return 2.

See also the section on the RANK function on page 69.

	A	B	C	D
158	RANK			
159				
160	ARG1	ARG2	ARG3	ARG4
161	25.00%	27.00%	15.00%	33.00%
162				
163	Order	Order		
164		1		
165				
166	Result	Result		
167	3	2		

Figure 7.12: Sample results of the ***RANK*** *function.*

Rank Function (RANK)

Syntax: RANK(number; set; order)

The `RANK` function returns the rank of a given number in the given set of numbers. You give it a value, a set, and `RANK` will tell you the given number is either 1st, 2nd, 3rd, and so on.

For example, if you wanted to know how your company's share of the market determines its place in that market, you'd use something like

```
=RANK(25%; A161:D161)
```

And `RANK` would return 3, indicating that your company is the third largest player on the market. You can reverse the order of the ranking if you use the third argument equal to `1` (descending), `0` is ascending, but you can omit that because it is a default value. For example:

```
=RANK(25%; A1:A4; 1)
```

would return 2, indicating that your company is the second smallest player on the market.

For more statistical functions click the **Function Wizard** button and choose **Statistical** from the **Categories** list.

Chapter 8

Calculations with Money

Although OpenOffice.org Calc's mathematical and statistical functions are advanced enough to construct any financial function you might need, you don't have to do it, because OpenOffice.org Calc ships with many built-in financial functions such as rates of return, future values of investments, and so on. And this chapter is all about them.

The financial functions can be divided into the following groups:

- Investment calculations.
- Asset depreciation.

Investment Calculations

Investment calculation functions are used to compute interest rates, payments, and the length of time needed to repay a loan. They are also a good tool to use to compare the profitability of various investments.

Cumulative Compounded Interest (CUMIPMT)

Syntax: CUMIPMT(interest; time; capital; start; end; type)

The CUMIPMT (cumulative compounded interest) function returns the amount of interest that needs to be paid on the principal or capital, borrowed for a period of time defined as the total number of payment periods (months, quarters, years, and so on).

It is assumed that the rate of interest remains constant for the whole accounting period. You can calculate the amount of interest to be paid back for the whole period or a part of it using the start and end arguments. For example, if you borrow $1,000,000 for 25 years at a constant rate of interest of 7.25% and want to know how much interest you need to pay in the first quarter of the first year, assuming monthly payments made at the beginning of each month, you need to use the following function:

```
=CUMIPMT(7.25%/12; 25*12; 1,000,000; 1; 3; 0)
```

The result is -$18,103.45.

It is necessary to divide the rate of interest and multiply the number of years by the number of months (or equivalent payment periods) to make sure that the calculations are correct. For quarterly payments, the function would look like this:

```
=CUMIPMT(7.25%/4; 25*4; 1,000,000; 1; 1; 0)
```

	A	B	C	D
169	CUMIPMT	INTEREST	TIME	CAPITAL
170	CUMIPMT	7.25%	25	$1,000,000
171				
172		START	END	TYPE
173		1	3	0
174				
175	Result			
176	-$18,103.45			

*Figure 8.1: Sample result of the **CUMIPMT** function.*

The fourth and fifth arguments (`start` and `end`) indicate the start and end payment periods for which the amount of compound interest is being calculated.

In the first example it was the first and the third month of the first year; in the second example it was the first quarter of the first year. The first month of the second year would be represented by 13, and the first quarter of the second year would be represented by 5.

The last argument, `type`, is used to tell OpenOffice.org Calc when payments are made: when money is paid at the beginning of each accounting period use 1, and if the payments are to be made at the end of each accounting period use 0.

- It is a generally accepted rule that we mark arguments and results with the minus sign (-) when they indicate money that needs to be paid out to somebody and without the minus sign when the money is received. OpenOffice.org Calc's functions do it automatically for the results but not for the arguments (however, OpenOffice.org Calc returns an error if you put a minus sign where it is not supposed to be.

- Also see the description of the CUMPRINC function, which calculates the amount of compound principal capital paid back over a given period of time.

- Always remember to put the right percentage values into functions that require them. There is a big difference between 10 (which OpenOffice.org Calc interprets as 1,000% or one thousand percent) and 10%.

	A	B	C	D
178	CUMPRINC	INTEREST	TIME	CAPITAL
179	CUMPRINC	7.25%	25	$1,000,000
180				
181		START	END	TYPE
182		1	3	0
183				
184	Result			
185	-$3,580.75			

*Figure 8.2: Sample result of the **CUMPRINC** function.*

Cumulative Principal Capital (CUMPRINC)

Syntax: CUMPRINC(interest; time; capital; start; end; type)

Complementary to the `CUMIPMT` function, `CUMPRINC` returns the amount of the compound principal capital that needs to be paid back within a given period of time defined as the total number of payment periods (months, quarters, years, and so on). It is assumed that the rate of interest remains constant for the whole accounting period.

This function is useful if you want to know how much of the principal capital borrowed needs to be paid back within the specified amount of time or any shorter interval specified by the `start` and `end` arguments.

For example, if you borrow `$1,000,000` for `25` years at a constant rate of interest of `7.25%` and want to know how much capital you need to return within the first quarter of the first year (assuming monthly payments made at the beginning of each month) you need to use the following function:

```
=CUMPPMT(7.25%/12; 25*12; 1,000,000; 1; 3; 0)
```

It is necessary to divide the rate of interest, and multiply the number of years, by the number of months (or equivalent payment periods) to make sure that the calculations are correct. For quarterly payments, the function would look like this:

```
=CUMPPMT(7.25%/4; 25*4; 1,000,000; 1; 1; 0)
```

The function returns -$3,605.44, which is more than -$3,605.44 from the previous example.

The fourth and fifth arguments (start and end) indicate the start and end payment periods for which the amount of compound capital is being calculated.

In the first example it was the first and the third month of the first year, in the second example it was the first quarter of the first year. The first month of the second year would have number 13 and the first quarter of the second year would have number 5.

If the payments are to be made at the beginning of each accounting period, use 1 instead of 0 as the last argument (type) of this function.

Also see the description of the CUMIPMT function, which calculates the amount of interest on principal capital to be paid back in a given amount of time.

Time to Maturity (DURATION)

Syntax: DURATION(interest; investment; future)

The DURATION function returns the number of periods (years if a yearly interest rate is used) for a given investment to reach the desired future value, assuming a constant rate of interest. For example, if you want to know how many years you have to wait for $1,000 deposited in a bank account that pays 3% interest annually for your money to become $2,000, use the following formula:

	A	B	C	D	E
187	DURATION	Interest	Investment	Future	Result
188	DURATION	3.00%	$1,000.00	$2,000.00	23.45

*Figure 8.3: Sample result of the **DURATION** function.*

```
=DURATION(3%; 1000; 2000)
```

The answer is, a long 23.45 years. If you want to see the answer given in whole years, without funny fractions, use the ROUNDUP function, as in

```
=ROUNDUP(DURATION(3%; 1000; 2000); 0)
```

	A	B	C	D
190	EFFECTIVE	Nominal	Periods	Result
191	EFFECTIVE	10.00%	12	10.47%

*Figure 8.4: Sample result of the **EFFECTIVE** function.*

Effective Rate of Interest (EFFECTIVE)

Syntax: EFFECTIVE(nominal; periods)

The EFFECTIVE function returns the effective annual rate of interest for the nominal rate of interest and the number of payment periods (typically months if the nominal rate is an annual rate). So, if you want to check the effective rate of interest for a nominal rate of 10%, assuming 12 monthly payments, use

```
=EFFECTIVE(10%; 12)
```

which returns 10.47%.

The opposite of this function is NOMINAL (page 81).

	A	B	C	D
193	FV	Interest	Time	Installment
194	FV	5.00%	25	-$100.00
195				
196		Deposit	Type	
197		-$10,000.00	0	
198				
199	Result			
200	$94,363.88			

Figure 8.5: Sample result of the ***FV*** *function.*

Future Value (FV)

Syntax: FV(interest; time; installment; deposit; type)

The FV function returns the future value of an initial lump `deposit` investment deposit followed by the given number of regular, equal installments made over a length of `time`, assuming a constant rate of `interest`.

The `time` argument specifies the total number of payments, and the `installment` argument is the amount of money paid each time.

For example, if you want to know how much money you could save if you paid $100 each month for 25 years into a savings account that pays a constant interest of 5%, you could use the following formula:

```
=FV(5%/12; 25*12; -100)
```

The answer is `$59,550.97`. Not bad at all. But how much could you save if you paid `$1,200` annually? Let's see:

```
=FV(5%; 25; -1,200)
```

returns `$57,272.52`.

Clearly, it is much more profitable to pay in smaller amounts but more frequently.

- Remember that the rate of interest ought to be followed by the percentage (%) sign and, for payments made more frequently than once per year, the rate of interest must be divided by the number of payments in a year. For monthly payments it means that the rate of interest is divided by 12, for quarterly payments the rate of interest is divided by 4, and so on.

- The time argument must be equal to the number of payments made. For example: for an investment in which contributions are made monthly for four years, you'd make time equal to 48 (4*12).

- In both of the previous calculations we assumed that you make deposits at the beginning of the accounting period. To calculate payments at the end of the accounting period, you need to use the fifth argument type, which can be set to 0 for payments made at the end of each accounting period or 1 for payments made at the beginning of each accounting period. If you use the fifth argument, you must also enter the fourth, deposit, as well, which is used to give the initial amount of savings.

The FV function may be used for some more complex calculations. You might want to know, for example, how much your current savings, say $10,000, will be worth in 25 years if you boost it with monthly payments of $100. Here you go:

```
=FV(5%/12; 25*12; -100; -10,000; 0)
```

The answer is a healthy $94,363.88 (payments made at the end of each accounting period, compared to an even nicer $94,612.00 when payments are made at the beginning of each accounting period.

- It is necessary to divide the rate of interest, and multiply the number of years, by the number of months (or equivalent payment periods) to make sure that the calculations are correct. The rate of interest is always assumed to be the annual rate of interest. Therefore, if you need to compute monthly payments, you need to divide the rate by 12 and multiply the number of years by 12, Similarly, if you were computing quarterly payments, you would

	A	B	C	D
202	IPMT	Interest	Period	Time
203	IPMT	7.25%	1	300
204				
205		Loan	Future	Type
206		$1,000,000.00	3	0
207				
208	Result			
209	-$6,041.67			

*Figure 8.6: Sample result of the **IPMT** function.*

divide the interest rate by 4 and multi- ply the number of years by 4.

See also the description of the PV function on page 87.

Interest (IPMT)

Syntax: IPMT(interest; period; time; loan; future; type)

The `IPMT` function returns the amount of interest that you need to pay in a given accounting `period` when you borrow a certain amount of money (`loan`) for a specified length of time. For example, if you borrow `$1,000,000` at an interest rate of `7.25%` for 25 years, and want to know how much interest you have to pay back within the first month, you can find that out with this formula:

```
=IPMT(7.25%/12; 1; 25*12; 1,000,000)
```

The answer is `-$6041.67`.

The `period` argument specifies for which accounting period the interest is going to be calculated and the `time` argument is equal to the number of accounting periods. The `future` argument is used to enter the amount of money remaining after the last payment is

	A	B
211	IRR	Flows
212	IRR	-$25,000.00
213		$30,000.00
214		$40,000.00
215		$28,000.00
216		$12,000.00
217	Result	
218	120.23%	

Figure 8.7: Sample result of the ***IRR*** *function.*

made. For loans, you usually enter 0 or don't use this argument at all unless you want to use the `type` argument as well, which is equal to 1 when payments are made at the beginning of each accounting period or equal to 0 when payments are made at the end of each accounting period.

`IPMT` is similar to `CUMIPMT`, but it calculates interest payable in a single accounting period whereas `CUMIPMT` calculates the compound interest for one or more accounting periods.

See also the sections on the `PPMT` (page 85) and `NPER` (page 82) functions.

Internal Rate of Return (IRR)

Syntax: IRR(cash_flows; guess)

The `IRR` function computes the internal rate of return for a given amount of initial investment and a series of cash flows. For example, if you invest `$25,000` in a coffee shop and want to know the internal rate of return for this investment based on the fact that you received `$30,000`, `$40,000`, `$28,000` and `$12,000` in return over four years, you should put `-$25,000` (the initial investment) into one cell and all of the income, without the minus sign, in cells below or to the right. If your values are in cells `B212:B216`, you can type the following formula:

	A	B	C	D
220	NOMINAL	Effective	Periods	Result
221	NOMINAL	10.47%	12	10.00%

Figure 8.8: Sample result of the ***NOMINAL*** *function.*

=IRR(B212:B216)

and the answer is 120.23%.

Not bad for a coffee shop. The guess argument is used to specify an estimated value of the internal rate of return for the given series of cash flows.

Nominal Rate of Interest (NOMINAL)

Syntax: NOMINAL(effective; periods)

The NOMINAL function returns the nominal rate of interest for a given effective rate of interest and the number of payments. So, if you want to check the nominal rate of interest for an effective rate of 10.47% assuming 12 payment per year, use =NOMINAL(10.47%; 12) which returns 10%.

☞ The opposite of this function is EFFECTIVE (page 76).

	A	B	C	D
223	NPER	Interest	Investment	Return
224	NPER	7.50%	-$10,000.00	$100,000.00
225				
226		Future	Type	
227				
228				
229	Result			
230	19.17			

*Figure 8.9: Sample result of the **NPER** function.*

Time to Repay a Loan (NPER)

Syntax: NPER(interest; installment; loan; future; type)

If you need an answer to a simple question such as “how many years should it take me to pay the money I borrowed, providing that I pay in equal chunks of money and the interest rate is constant?”, the NPER function is the right tool to use. Consider the following case: you borrow $100,000 (loan) at an annual rate of interest equal to 7.5%, and you want to pay back $10,000 each year. To see how many years it would take you to do this, use this formula:

```
=NPER(7.5%; -10,000; 100,000)
```

which returns, in this case, 19.17 years!

The future argument is used to enter the amount of money remaining after the last payment is made. For loans, you usually enter 0 or don’t use this argument at all unless you want to use the type argument as well, which is equal to 1 when payments are made at the beginning of each accounting period or equal to 0 when payments are made at the end of each accounting period.

See also the sections on the IPMT and PPMT functions.

	A	B	C	D
232	NPV	Investment	Discount	Flows
233	NPV	-$25,000.00	10.00%	$30,000.00
234				$40,000.00
235				$28,000.00
236				$12,000.00
237				
238	Result			
239	$64,563.55			

Figure 8.10: Sample result of the ***NPV*** *function.*

Net Present Value (NPV)

Syntax: NPV(discount; value1; value2; ... value30)

The NPV function returns the Net Present Value of an investment. Consider the coffee shop example discussed previously in connection with the IRR function.

To calculate the value of the investment after four years, you need to put into the NPV function the discount rate (such as inflation) and the cash flows for each year. Then, subtract the initial investment from the result of the NPV.

Let's assume that income flows are stored in cells D233:D237 and the initial investment, a negative value, is stored in cell B233:

```
=NPV(10%; D233:D237)+B233
```

This returns $64,563.55.

The initial investment ought to be subtracted from the received income, but we are adding it because it is a negative value according to OpenOffice.org Calc's convention of marking money paid out as negative with the minus (-) sign and money received as positive (no minus sign).

	A	B	C	D
241	PMT	Interest	Time	Loan
242	PMT	7.50%	25	-$1,000,000.00
243				
244		Future	Type	
245				
246				
247	Result			
248	$75,000.00			

Figure 8.11: Sample result of the ***PMT*** *function.*

Now you know how hard your money is working. Another important case is accounting for loss. For example: if your little coffee shop made a loss of `$3,000` in the fifth year, and then a profit of `$20,000` in the sixth year, you'd need to account for that in the following way:

```
=NPV(10%; D233:D237; -3,000; 20,000)+B233
```

And the answer would be `$73,990.27`.

Although it is possible to insert the initial investment into the `NPV` function as a negative value, you shouldn't be really doing that as this is only valid in cases when we invest at the end of the first accounting period, hardly a typical case, because this assumes that our business venture is running for the first year without any money.

Payment (PMT)

Syntax: PMT(interest; time; loan; future; type)

Wondering how much you would have to pay monthly for your mortgage if you agreed to constant monthly repayments? The `PMT` function is the right tool to use:

```
=PMT(7.5%/12; 25*12; 1,000,000)
```

In this case you assume that you borrow a cool $1,000,000 (the loan) at a constant interest rate of 7.5% and you would be paying it back over 25 years. If that's the situation, your monthly rate would be -$7,389.91. The minus sign indicates that this is the money paid out of your pocket.

- The first argument is the annual interest rate which must be divided by 12 if you are making monthly payments, by 4 if payments are made every quarter, or by 2 if payments are made twice a year.
- The second argument, time, is the total number of payments to be made.
- The third argument is the present value of the loan.
- The last two arguments are the future balance after the last payment is made and the type of payments (0 indicates that payments are made at the end of each accounting period, and 1 indicates that payments are made at the beginning of each accounting period).
- See also the sections on the EFFECTIVE (page 76), IPMT (page 79), NOMINAL (page 81), and PPMT (page 85) functions.

Capital (PPMT)

Syntax: PPMT(interest; period; time; loan; future; type)

The PPMT function returns the amount of original capital that you need to pay back in a given accounting period when you borrow money. For example, if you borrow $1,000,000 (loan) at an interest rate of 7.25% for 25 years, and want to know how much

	A	B	C	D
250	PPMT	Interest	Period	Time
251	PPMT	7.25%	1	300
252				
253		Loan	Future	Type
254		$1,000,000.00		
255				
256	Result			
257	-$1,186.40			

*Figure 8.12: Sample result of the **PPMT** function.*

capital you have to pay back within the first month, you can find that out with this formula:

```
=IPMT(7.25%/12; 1; 25*12; 1,000,000)
```

The answer is `-$1,186.40`.

- The `interest` argument is the interest rate at which money is borrowed.
- The `period` argument is the number of the chosen accounting period, and the `time` argument is the total number of accounting periods.
- The present value of a loan is given as the `loan` argument.
- The `future` argument is used to enter the amount of money remaining after the last payment is made. For loans, you usually enter `0` or don't use this argument at all unless you want to use the `type` argument as well, which is equal to `1` when payments are made at the beginning of each accounting period or equal to `0` when payments are made at the end of each accounting period.

This function is similar to `CUMPRINC` but calculates the amount of capital that needs to be paid in a single accounting period, and `CUMPRINC` calculates the amount of capital that needs to be paid in one or more accounting periods. See also the section on the `IPMT` function.

This function was known as `IPMT` in StarOffice 5.0 (predecessor to OpenOffice.org). Make sure that the StarOffice Calc 5.0 documents imported into OpenOffice.org Calc contain correct functions.

	A	B	C	D
259	PV	Interest	Time	Installment
260	PV	5.00%	25	-$100.00
261				
262		Deposit	Type	
263		$0.00	0	
264				
265	Result			
266	$17,106.00			

*Figure 8.13: Sample result of the **PV** function.*

Present Value (PV)

Syntax: PV(interest; time; installment; future; type)

The PV function presents the value of an investment. This function returns present value of a series of installments. For example: if you are saving $100 each month for 25 years and the interest rate is going to be a constant 5%, your future savings are now worth:

```
=PV(5%/12; 25*12; -100)
```

which is $17,106.00.

- The `interest` argument is the annual interest rate (must be divided by 12 if payments are made monthly, or by 4 if payments are made quarterly), the `time` argument is the total number of payment periods.
- The `installment` is the amount of money paid at the beginning or the end of each accounting period.
- The `future` argument is used to enter the amount of money remaining after the last payment is made. For loans, you usually enter 0 or don't use this argument at all unless you want to use the `type` argument as well, which is equal to 1 when payments are made at the beginning of each

	A	B	C	D
268	RATE	Time	Installment	Investment
269	RATE	25	-$100,000.00	$1,000,000.00
270				
271		Deposit	Type	
272				
273				
274	Result			
275	8.78%			

*Figure 8.14: Sample result of the **RATE** function.*

accounting period or equal to 0 when payments are made at the end of each accounting period.

See also the section on the FV function on page 77.

Annual Rate of Interest for Loans (RATE)

Syntax: RATE(time; installment; investment; future; type)

Suppose you want to borrow `$1,000,000` and repay it in lump sums of `$100,000` over 25 years. What annual interest rate should the lender set? To find out the answer to a question such as that, use

```
=RATE(25; -100000; 1,000,000)
```

and you see that it would be at least `8.78%`.

- Do not forget to add a minus sign (-) in front of the payment to indicate the money paid out.

- The `future` argument is used to enter the amount of money remaining after the last payment is made. For loans, you usually enter 0 or don't use this argument at all unless

	A	B	C	D	E
277	ZGZ	Time	Value	Future Value	Result
278	ZGZ	25	100000	1000000	#REF!

Figure 8.15: Sample result of the ***ZGZ*** *function.*

you want to use the type argument as well, which is equal to 1 when payments are made at the beginning of each accounting period or equal to 0 when payments are made at the end of each accounting period.

Annual Rate of Interest for Savings (ZGZ)

Syntax: ZGZ(time; value; future)

What should be the interest rate if you want your investment of, say `$100,000`, to turn into a nice and round `$1,000,000` over 25 years?

`=ZGZ(25; 100,000; 1,000,000)`

The answer is `9.65%`.

Asset Depreciation

Use these functions to compute depreciation and amortization of assets.

Declining Balance Method (DB)

Syntax: DB(cost; salvage; life; period; months)

If you want to use the fixed-declining balance method for calculation of depreciation of assets, this is the function to use. It answers questions such as "what is the depreciation in year x," even

	A	B	C	D
280	DB	Cost	Salvage	Life
281	DB	$1,000,000.00	$100.00	4
282				
283		Period	Months	
284		2	8	
285				
286	Result			
287	$360,000.00			

*Figure 8.16: Sample result of the **DB** function.*

if you bought that asset sometime in the middle of the year. For example: when you buy an asset worth $1,000,000 with a life of 4 years at the beginning of May, you can find its depreciation in year 2 using

```
=DB(1,000,000; 100; 4; 2; 8)
```

The answer is $360,000.00.

- The first argument, `cost`, is the price you pay for the asset.
- The second, `salvage`, is how much you can get for it (in the preceding example it was $100) when you sell it after a certain number of accounting periods (`life`—for yearly depreciation insert the number of years, for monthly—months, and so on).
- The `period` argument is the accounting period you are trying to find depreciation for and the `months` argument it is the number of months left in the year you bought the asset (the first year, so even when you buy an asset with a life of 4 years at the beginning of December, you put 4 into the `life` and 1 into the `month` argument).

	A	B	C	D
289	DDB	Cost	Salvage	Life
290	DDB	$1,000,000.00	$100.00	4
291				
292		Period	Months	
293		2	2	
294				
295	Result			
296	$250,000.00			

*Figure 8.17: Sample result of the **DDB** function.*

Double-Declining Balance Method (DDB)

Syntax: DDB(cost; salvage; life; period; factor)

This function is similar to `DB`, only it uses the double-declining balance method and lets you set your own depreciation factor, which is set by default to 2. Using similar data as in the section on the `DB` function, we get these results:

```
=DDB(1,000,000; 100; 4; 2; 2)
```

The answer is `$250,000.00`, but if you change the factor to 3, as in

```
=DDB(1,000,000; 100; 4; 2; 3)
```

the result is `$187,500.00`.

- The first argument, `cost`, is the price you pay for the asset.
- The second, `salvage`, is how much you can get for it (in the preceding example it was `$100`) when you sell it after a certain number of accounting periods (`life`—for yearly depreciation insert the number of years, for monthly, months, and so on).

	A	B	C	D	E
298	SLN	Cost	Salvage	Life	Result
299	SLN	$1,000,000.00	$1.00	$3.00	$333,333.00

*Figure 8.18: Sample result of the **SLN** function.*

- The `period` argument is the accounting period you are trying to find depreciation for.
- See also the section on the VDB function on page 94.

Straight Line Depreciation (SLN)

Syntax: SLN(cost; salvage; life)

The SLN function returns the straight line depreciation of an asset for the life of that asset. For example: if you have just bought a brand new Cray supercomputer for our favorite amount of cash, $1,000,000, and you know that in three years it should be worth a nice $1.00, the value of

```
=SLN(1,000,000; 1; 3)
```

The result is $333,333.00 which you might even be able to write off!

The first argument, `cost`, is the price you pay for the asset. The second, `salvage`, is how much you can get for it (in the preceding example it was $1) when you sell it after a certain number of accounting periods (the `life` argument—for yearly depreciation insert the number of years, for monthly, months, and so on).

	A	B	C	D	E
301	SYD	Cost	Salvage	Life	Period
302	SYD	$1,000,000.00	$100.00	4	2
303					
304	Result				
305	$299,970.00				

*Figure 8.19: Sample result of the **SYD** function.*

Sum-of-Years Method (SYD)

Syntax: SYD(cost; salvage; life; period)

This function gives asset depreciation using the sum-of-years-digits method. For example

```
=SLN(1,000,000; 100; 4; 2)
```

is equal to `$299,970.00`.

- The first argument, `cost`, is the price you pay for the asset.
- The second, `salvage`, is how much you can get for it (in the preceding example it was $100) when you sell it after a certain number of accounting periods (the `life` argument —for yearly depreciation insert the number of years, for monthly, months, and so on).
- The `period` argument is the accounting period you are trying to find depreciation for.

	A	B	C	D	E
301	VDB	Cost	Salvage	Life	Start Period
302	VDB	$1,000,000.00	$100.00	4	2
303					
304		End Period	Factor	No Switch	
305		3	1	0	
306					
307	Result				
308	$249,966.67				

Figure 8.20: Sample result of the ***VDB*** *function.*

Double Declining Curve Method (VDB)

Syntax: VDB(cost; salvage; life; start_period; end_period; factor; no_switch)

Asset depreciation for a given period or partial period using the double declining curve is given by this function. This function is similar to `DDB` and lets you set your own depreciation factor (default value is 2).

Unlike `DDB`, `VDB` enables you to compute depreciation for more than one accounting period. Using similar data as in the section on the `DDB` function, we get these results:

```
=VDB(1,000,000; 100; 4; 2; 3; 1; 0)
```

which is equal to `$249,966.67`.

- The first argument, `cost`, is the price you pay for the asset.
- The second, `salvage`, is how much you can get for it (in the preceding example it was `$100`) when you sell it after a certain number of accounting periods (the `life` argument —for yearly depreciation insert the number of years, for monthly, months, and so on).

- The `start_period` and `end_period` arguments are used to specify the first and last accounting period used in calculations.

- The last two arguments, `factor` and `no_switch`, are used to specify your own depreciation factor and tell OpenOffice.org Calc if you want it to automatically switch to the straight line depreciation method when the depreciation is larger than the value it was calculated for (`no_switch` argument, default value 0).

- See also the section on the DDB function on page 91.

Chapter 9

Text Functions

OpenOffice.org Calc can process all sorts of data, including text. The following functions help you do anything you like with strings of text, including turning numbers into text, splitting, splicing, searching, and replacing.

The arguments of these functions, all strings must be enclosed in double quotes (").

The following text functions are described in the next sections:

- Formatting functions.
- Conversion functions.
- Search and replace functions.
- Utility functions.

Formatting Functions

These functions are used to format text that might be formatted in a way that does not suit your needs. You can join, divide, search, and replace parts of text and numbers with these functions.

	A	B	C	D	E
310	CONCATENATE	Text1	Text2	Text3	Result
311	CONCATENATE	Bonnie		Clyde	Bonnie Clyde

Figure 9.1: Sample result of the ***CONCATENATE*** *function.*

Join Strings of Text (& or CONCATENATE)

Syntax: & or CONCATENATE(text1; text2; ... text30)

The `CONCATENATE` function can join up to 30 strings of text. There is no limit for the & operator. For example:

`="Bonnie"&"Clyde"`

becomes `BonnieClyde`.

If you want to add spaces you need to use a space enclosed in parentheses (""). For example:

`="Bonnie"&" "&"Clyde"`

returns `Bonnie Clyde`.

If these strings were stored in three separate cells, you could also use this notation

`=A1&A2&A3`

or

`=CONCATENATE(B311;C311;D311)`

assuming that `B311` holds `"Bonnie"`, `C311` holds `" "` and `D311` holds `"Clyde"`.

	A	B	C
313	CLEAN	Text	Result
314	CLEAN	♫♪	

Figure 9.2: Sample result of the ***CLEAN*** *function.*

CLEAN

Syntax: CLEAN(text)

Removes the non-printable characters from the `text` string. It is useful for cleaning up database files, especially those imported from other operating systems.

	A	B	C
316	LOWER	Text	Result
317	LOWER	OpenOffice.org	openoffice.org

Figure 9.3: Sample result of the ***LOWER*** *function.*

LOWER

Syntax: LOWER(text)

This function turns all given characters into lowercase. For example:

```
=LOWER("OpenOffice.org")
```

returns `openoffice.org`.

☞ See also the section on the UPPER function on page 101.

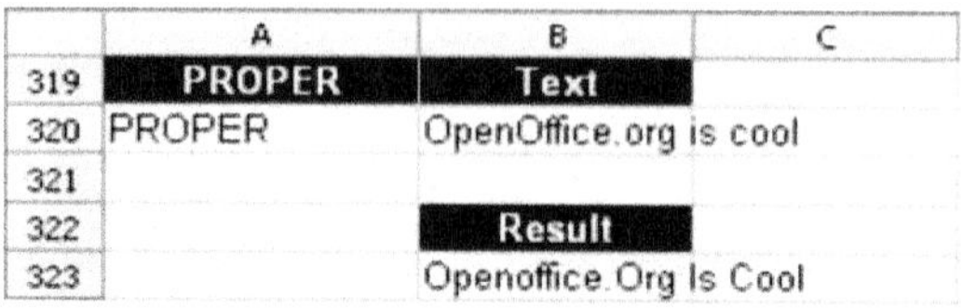

	A	B	C
319	PROPER	Text	
320	PROPER	OpenOffice.org is cool	
321			
322		Result	
323		Openoffice.Org Is Cool	

Figure 9.4: Sample result of the ***PROPER*** *function.*

PROPER

Syntax: PROPER(text)

The `PROPER` function capitalizes the first letter in every word in the given string. For example:

```
=PROPER("openoffice.org is cool")
```

returns `OpenOffice.org  Office Is Cool.`

See also the sections on the `LOWER` (page 99) and `UPPER` (page 101) functions.

TEXT

Syntax: TEXT(number; format)

This function returns a given number as a text string formatted according to the given numeric format. Designing your own format is described in Chapter 4 on page 25. If you already have a numeric format that you like, simply copy it from the **Format Code** field in the **Cells Format** dialog box into the **Format** field in the **Function Wizard**.

Always remember to put the format string inside double quotes as in this example:

```
=TEXT(-1000000; "[$$-409]#,##0.00;[RED]-[$
$-409]#,##0.00")
```

which returns `-$1,000,000.00.`

	A	B	C
325	TRIM	Text	
326	TRIM	OpenOffice.org is cool	
327			
328		Result	
329		OpenOffice.org is cool	

*Figure 9.5: Sample result of the **TRIM** function.*

TRIM

Syntax: TRIM(text)

This function removes extra spaces from strings. For example:

`=TRIM("OpenOffice.org      is      Cool!")`

returns `OpenOffice.org is Cool!`.

	A	B	C
331	UPPER	Text	
332	UPPER	OpenOffice.org	
333			
334		Result	
335		OPENOFFICE.ORG	

*Figure 9.6: Sample results of the **FACT** function.*

UPPER

Syntax: UPPER(text)

Upper turns all characters into uppercase. For example:

`=UPPER("OpenOffice.org")`

returns `OPENOFFICE.ORG`.

See also `LOWER` (page 99).

Chapter 10

Conversion Functions

Text conversion functions convert numbers into strings and vice-versa. They are useful for generating strings of text that contain numbers in a specific format.

Converting Between Numeric Systems (BASE)

Syntax: BASE(number; base; min_length)

This function converts numbers into text strings that represent the numbers in a different numeric system. It is useful for turning decimal numbers into binary, octal, and hexadecimal numbers. For example:

```
=BASE(12; 2; 16)
```

	A	B	C	D
337	BASE	Number	Base	Min Length
338	BASE	12	2	16
339				
340	Result			
341		0000000000001100		

*Figure 10.1: Sample result of the **BASE** function.*

turns number 12 into the string 0000000000001100 (binary number), while

`=BASE(12; 8; 16)`

turns number 12 into the string 0000000000000014 (octal number), and

`=BASE(12; 16; 16)`

turns 12 into the string 000000000000000C (hexadecimal number).

As you can see, it is possible to specify the minimum length using the third parameter of the generated string, and the empty spaces are filled with zeroes.

The `base` argument can be any number from 2 to 36.

Converting Numbers into Currency Strings (DOLLAR)

Syntax: DOLLAR(value; decimal_places)

The `DOLLAR` function converts the given `value` into text in currency format. For example:

	A	B	C	D
343	DOLLAR	Value	Dec. Places	Result
344	DOLLAR	1000000	2	$1,000,000.00

Figure 10.2: Sample result of the ***DOLLAR*** *function.*

`=DOLLAR(1,000,000; 2)`

returns `$1,000,000.00`.

The second argument indicates the number of places past the decimal point. Why would it be important at all? Well, it is good for making headlines such as `A Cool $1,000,000.00 in Sales!`, which you could code as:

`="A cool "&DOLLAR(1,000,000; 2)&" in Sales!"`

	A	B	C	D
346	FIXED	Value	Dec. Places	Result
347	FIXED	1000000	2	1,000,000.00

Figure 10.3: Sample result of the ***FIXED*** *function.*

Adding Thousand Separators (FIXED)

Syntax: FIXED(number, decimal_places; no_commas)

The `FIXED` function converts the given number into comma-separated text format. For example:

`=FIXED(1000000; 2)`

returns `1,000,000.00` unless you put `1` as the third argument to switch commas off.

	A	B	C	D
349	FIND	Pattern	Text	Result
350	FIND	Office	OpenOffice.org	5

Figure 10.4: Sample result of the ***FIND*** *function.*

The second argument, `decimal_places` is used to specify the number of decimal places. For an idea on how to use this function see `DOLLAR`.

Search and Replace Functions

Search and replace functions enable us to modify strings of text and extract numbers, words, and other elements from them.

Searching for Strings (FIND – Case-Sensitive)

Syntax: FIND(find_text; source_text; start_from)

This function finds the starting position of the specified text string (`find_text`) within another text string (`source_text`). For example:

```
=FIND("Office"; "OpenOffice.org")
```

returns 5, the starting position of the `Office` string within the `OpenOffice.org` string.

The third, optional argument start_from, is used to specify the starting position within `source_text` from which `FIND` begins looking for the `find_text` string.

	A	B	C	D
352	REPLACE	Old Text	Start	Number
353	REPLACE	OpenOffice.org	5	10
354				
355		Replacement		Result
356		Calc		OpenCalc

*Figure 10.5: Sample result of the **REPLACE** function.*

Replacing Strings (REPLACE)

Syntax: REPLACE(old_text; start_number; number_of_chars; new_text)

This function replaces part of a string `old_text` with a new string `new_text`, as in

```
=REPLACE("OpenOffice.org"; 5; 10; "Calc")
```

which returns `OpenCalc`.

The two numeric arguments (`start_number` and `number_of_chars`) are the position where the replacement ought to begin and the number of characters that are to be replaced.

	A	B	C	D
358	SEARCH	Pattern	Text	Result
359	SEARCH	office	OpenOffice.org	5

*Figure 10.6: Sample result of the **SEARCH** function.*

Searching for Strings (SEARCH – Case-Insensitive)

Syntax: SEARCH(find_text; source_text; start_number)

The `SEARCH` function finds the specified text string, `find_text`, within another text string, `source_text`, but unlike `FIND`, this

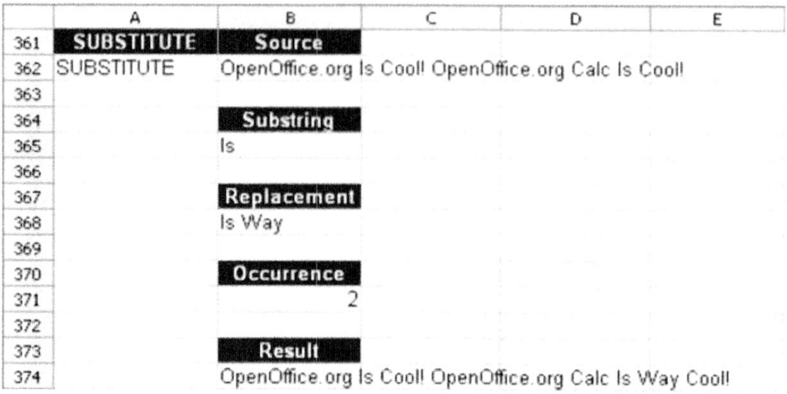

Figure 10.7: Sample result of the ***SUBSTITUTE*** *function.*

function is not case-sensitive. For example:

```
=FIND("office"; "OpenOffice.org")
```

returns error `#VALUE!`, but

```
=SEARCH("office"; "OpenOffice.org")
```

returns 5, the starting position of the `Office` string within the `OpenOffice.org` string.

The `start_number` argument enables you to change the position from which the search begins (default value is 1).

Selectively Replacing Strings (SUBSTITUTE)

Syntax: SUBSTITUTE(source_text; substring; new_text; occurrence)

The `SUBSTITUTE` function is similar to `REPLACE`, only here you can choose which occurrence of `substring` is to be replaced. For example:

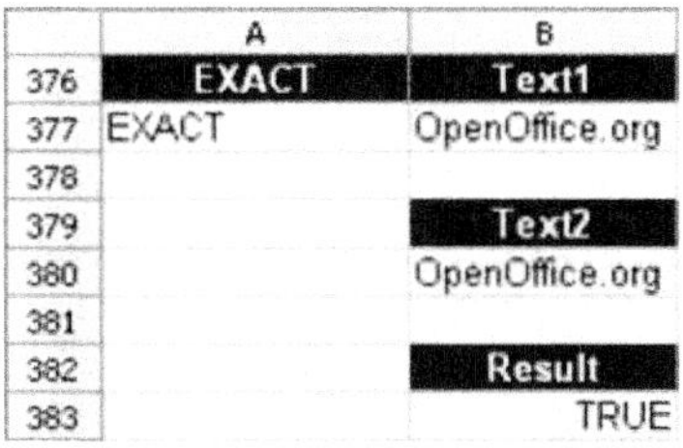

	A	B
376	EXACT	Text1
377	EXACT	OpenOffice.org
378		
379		Text2
380		OpenOffice.org
381		
382		Result
383		TRUE

Figure 10.8: Sample result of the ***EXACT*** *function.*

```
=SUBSTITUTE("OpenOffice.org Is Cool! OpenOffice.org
Calc Is Cool!"; "Is"; "Is Way"; 2)
```

returns

```
OpenOffice.org Is Cool! OpenOffice.org Calc Is Way
Cool!
```

The `source_text` argument is the text string where you need to find a substring to be replaced with `new_text`. The `occurrence` argument is used to specify which `substring` ought to be replaced.

Conditional Functions

Conditional functions are used to add some built-in "artificial intelligence" to your worksheets. They compare text strings and their results (`true` or `false`) can be used to change the appearance of the worksheet or the way calculations are done.

Comparing Strings (EXACT)

Syntax: EXACT(t1; t2)

EXACT compares two strings and returns 1 if they are exactly the same or 0 if they are not. For example

```
=EXACT("OpenOffice.org"; "OpenOffice.org")
```

returns 1, while

```
=EXACT("OpenOffice.org"; "openoffice.org")
```

returns 0.

Chapter 11

Utility Functions

Utility functions discussed in this chapter are used to perform various formatting chores and return useful information about text strings. They can help you in analysis of textual data, making OpenOffice.org Calc an even more useful tool.

	A	B	C
385	CHAR	Number	Result
386	CHAR	64	@

Figure 11.1: Sample result of the ***CHAR*** *function.*

ASCII Character (CHAR)

Syntax: CHAR(number)

The `CHAR` function returns an ASCII character whose `number` is 0 to 255. For example:

	A	B	C
388	CODE	Number	Result
389	CODE	OpenOffice.org	79

Figure 11.2: Sample result of the ***CODE*** *function.*

=CHAR(64)

returns the character @.

The characters displayed on screen may differ depending on the system's language and display font settings.

ASCII Code (CODE)

Syntax: CODE(text)

The CODE function returns the code of the first character in the given string. For example:

=CODE("OpenOffice.org")

returns 32.

Left-Side Substring (LEFT)

Syntax: LEFT(text; n)

The LEFT function returns the first character from the string text, or a specified number of n characters starting from the left. For example:

	A	B	C	D
391	LEFT	Text	N	Result
392	LEFT	OpenOffice.org	4	Open

*Figure 11.3: Sample result of the **LEFT** function.*

```
=LEFT("OpenOffice.org")
```

returns O, and

```
=LEFT("OpenOffice.org"; 4)
```

returns Open.

See also MID and RIGHT.

	A	B	C
394	LEN	Text	Result
395	LEN	OpenOffice.org	14

*Figure 11.4: Sample result of the **LEN** function.*

Length of a String (LEN)

Syntax: LEN(text)

The LEN function returns the length of the given string. For example:

```
=LEN("OpenOffice.org")
```

returns 14.

	A	B	C	D
397	MID	Text	Start	N
398	MID	OpenOffice.org	2	6
399				
400	Result			
401	penOff			

*Figure 11.5: Sample results of the **MID** function.*

Middle (MID)

Syntax: MID(text; start; n)

The `MID` function returns a substring of the `text` string, starting from the `start` position and containing a given number of characters (n). For example:

```
=MID("OpenOffice.org"; 2; 6)
```

returns `penOff`.

See also `LEFT` (page 112) and `RIGHT` (page 115).

	A	B	C	D
403	REPT	Text	N	Result
404	REPT	Op	4	OpOpOpOp

*Figure 11.6: Sample results of the **FACT** function.*

Repeat String (REPT)

Syntax: REPT(text; repetitions)

The `REPT` function creates a string that consists of a given string (`text`) repeated (n) number of times. For example:

	A	B	C	D
406	RIGHT	Text	N	Result
407	RIGHT	OpenOffice.org	4	.org

*Figure 11.7: Sample results of the **RIGHT** function.*

=REPT("Open"; 4)

returns OpenOpenOpenOpen.

Right-Side Substring (RIGHT)

Syntax: RIGHT(text; n)

The RIGHT function returns the last n characters from the end of the string text, or a specified number of characters (n) starting from the right. For example:

=RIGHT("OpenOffice.org", 4)

returns .org and

=RIGHT("OpenOffice.org"; 6)

returns ce.org.

See also LEFT (page 112) and MID (page 114).

	A	B	C
409	ROT13	Text	Result
410	ROT13	OpenOffice.org	BcraBssvpr.bet

*Figure 11.8: Sample results of the **ROT13** function.*

Obfuscate (ROT13)

Syntax: ROT13(text)

The `ROT13` function encrypts text using a simple algorithm called Ceasar's Code, where each letter is replaced by another one 13 characters away in the latin alphabet.

Rotating the encoded text by 13 again returns the original string. For example,

`=ROT13("OpenOffice.org")`

returns `BcraBssvpr.bet` while

`=ROT13(ROT13("OpenOffice.org"))`

returns `OpenOffice.org`.

It is not a very strong form of protecting data, but it is enough to keep it from being accidentally revealed to someone who might be "just looking".

	A	B	C
412	T	Text	Result
413	T	OpenOffice.org	OpenOffice.org

*Figure 11.9: Sample results of the **T** function.*

Return Text Values Only (T)

Syntax: T(value)

The T function is a bit strange. It returns the text string given to it as its argument. For example:

```
=T("OpenOffice.org")
```

returns `OpenOffice.org`, but

```
=T(10)
```

returns `""` because 10 is not a text string.

This function is obsolete and it is here only because of compatibility requirements with the old spreadsheet software.

Chapter 12

Time & Date Functions

We all know what dates are and what we mean when we say "I need it done in three days," but such natural expressions are not so easy for computers. Unfortunately, unlike other hard problems in life, computations that involve time and data are essential in business and cannot be ignored. Without them it would be very difficult to judge the potential profitability of a planned business venture, the real cost of a loan, or the future value of an investment.

A lot of financial functions greatly benefit from the use of date functions, because they make it possible to automate a lot of time-based calculations. And automating things is always a good idea, because it saves you time and money.

There are two kinds of OpenOffice.org Calc time-related functions: "date" functions (for bigger chunks of time: days, weeks, months, or years) and "time" functions (shorter periods of time like hours, minutes, or seconds). That distinction exists for your own comfort only, because all date and time calculations in OpenOffice.org Calc are based on the same fractional number aka. *timestamp* that

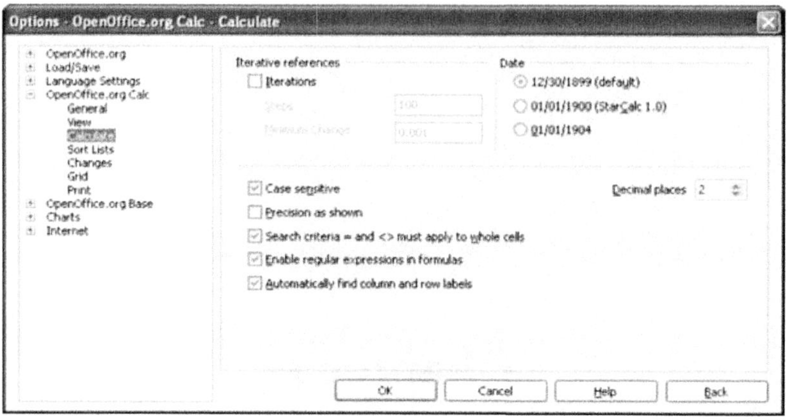

Figure 12.1: Set the Epoch in the Date section.

represents the number of seconds that have elapsed since a subjectively chosen moment in time called an Epoch, which is a fancy way of saying the time counter value was equal to 00:00:00.00 (i.e. zero).

You can set the Epoch yourself (choose **Tools ⇨ Options** and select the **Calculate** item in the **OpenOffice.org Calc** branch to display a panel where you can choose one of the three available Epochs (see the **Date** section in Figure 12.1).

Unless you have old documents created well before year 2000, you should always use the default Epoch of 12/30/1899.

Whichever Epoch you choose, the count starts at midnight. For the standard Epoch, OpenOffice.org Calc can recognize years between 1583 and 9956, or, if you enter them as two-digit years, from 19XX to 20XX–1.If you decide to use the shorter notation, i.e.. 12/15/20 instead of 12/15/2020, you will have to tell OpenOffice.org Calc how it ought to convert two-digit years into four-digit years.

You do it in the **Options** dialog box in the **General** branch (choose **Tools ⇨ Options**) as shown in Figure 12.2.

When you change Epochs or the two-year conversion settings, always do it before opening or creating a worksheet to make sure that the dates are interpreted in a consistent manner.

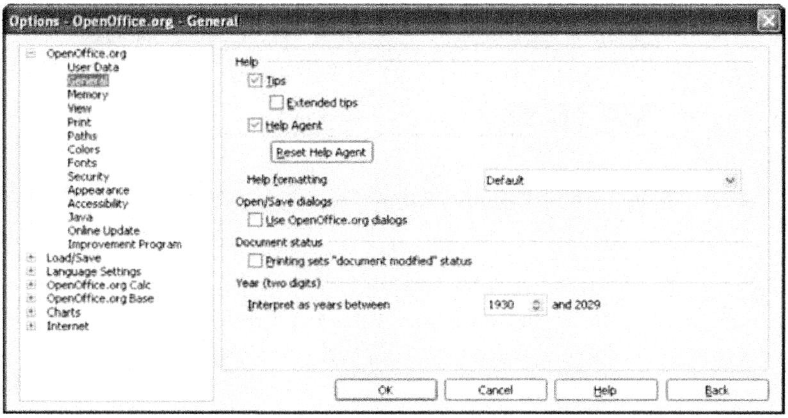

Figure 12.2: Set two-digit years in the Year section.

The date functions can be divided into the following groups:

- Functions that return a timestamp.
- Functions that extract date components
- Functions that calculate the difference between dates.

Functions that Return a Timestamp

Date and time information is stored on on modern computer systems as a fractional number called a *timestamp*. It is commonly set to the number of seconds that have elapsed from midnight January 1, 1970.

All date and time calculations are done much faster on timestamps than the date or time written the way we are used to, because a single number is easier to process. For example, to find out the difference between two dates it is sufficient to subtract two timestamps instead of comparing six numbers (two years, two months, two days).

	A	B	C	D
415	DATE	Year	Month	Day
416	DATE	2010	1	1
417				
418	Result			
419	40179			

Figure 12.3: Sample result of the ***DATE*** *function.*

To make it easy to work with timestamps, we need some helper functions like DATE. They are less often used today than a few years ago thanks to the maturity of the OpenOffice.org Calc code.

Timestamp (DATE)

Syntax: DATE(year; month; day)

The DATE function returns the timestamp for the given year, month, and day. To test it, place the following formula into any empty cell on the current worksheet:

```
=DATE(2010; 1; 1)
```

The result ought to be 40179.

If you see a date like 01/01/10, which is not what you wanted in this case, change the numeric formatting of that cell to **General**. In order to do that choose **Format ⇨ Cells** and click on the **Numbers** tab to change the numeric format for that cell to **Text / @**. The value of the timestamp might be different if you use a non-standard Epoch.

One useful trick that you might want to remember is using the DATE function to automatically calculate the timestamp of a day in a year's time. For example,

```
=DATE((YEAR(TODAY())+1); MONTH(TODAY());
DAY(TODAY()))
```

The formula shown above is useful if you are trying to do financial and other calculations based on time.

	A	B
421	**TODAY**	**Result**
422	TODAY	12/16/09

*Figure 12.4: Sample result of the **TODAY** function.*

Today's Timestamp (TODAY)

Syntax: TODAY()

This useful function returns the timestamp of the current day. For example, on January 3, 2010:

```
=TODAY()
```

returns `40181`.

You can use this function in a worksheet that calculates mortgage payment schedules for your clients. Instead of typing in a new date into a formula calculating mortgage payments, put TODAY into the start date values and it will save you a lot of time. You can be even more inventive and add or subtract a certain number of days to construct even more flexible formulas:

```
=TODAY()+30
```

The formula show above will regenerate the timestamp for a date 30 days from today. If you replace the hard number with a cell reference (e.g. A2), you will make the formula even more flexible, because you will not have to rewrite it every time you change the number of days you want to add or subtract:

```
=TODAY()+A2
```

See also the descriptions of financial functions such as FV and PV in the "Investment Calculations" chapter on page 72 for an example on how to use TODAY.

	A	B	C
424	DAY	Timestamp	Result
425	DAY	40179	1

*Figure 12.5: Sample result of the **DAY** function.*

Extracting Date Components

Some date and time operations are surprisingly inconvenient for humans. For example, if you ever had to find out the week number for a date you know how time-consuming such a simple task can be. The following functions help with such mundane tasks.

Extracting Days from a Date (DAY)

Syntax: DAY(t)

The `DAY` function is used to convert a date given in any recognizable format into a day of the month. For example:

```
=DAY(40179)
```

returns 1 (January 1, 2010).

You can give `DAY` the date in a more natural format, e.g.:

```
=DAY("3/17/2010")
```

returns 17 (March 17, 2010).

See the description of the `DATE` (page 122) function for another example of using the `DAY` function in practice.

	A	B	C
427	WEEKDAY	Date	Result
428	WEEKDAY	01/01/10	6

*Figure 12.6: Sample result of the **WEEKDAY** function.*

Extracting Weekdays from a Date (WEEKDAY)

Syntax: WEEKDAY(t; day)

The `WEEKDAY` function is used to convert a date given in any recognizable format into a day of the week. Days are numbered from 0 (Sunday) to 6 (Saturday). For example:

```
=WEEKDAY("1/1/2010")
```

returns 6.

The result shown above is produced by `WEEKDAY` assuming that weeks start on Sunday (day 0).

You can modify those results with the `day` argument. Its values can be as follows:

- 1 — weeks start on Sunday (day 0).
- 2 — weeks start on Monday (day 1).
- 3 — weeks start on Monday (day 0).

Compare the following formulas and their results for the same date:

```
=WEEKDAY("1/1/2010"; 1)
```

returns 6.

```
=WEEKDAY("1/1/2010"; 2)
```

returns 5.

	A	B	C
430	WEEKNUM	Date	Result
431	WEEKNUM	02/07/10	6

Figure 12.7: Sample result of the ***WEEKNUM*** *function.*

```
=WEEKDAY("1/1/2010"; 3)
```

returns 4.

Extract Week Number from a Date (WEEKNUM)

Syntax: WEEKNUM(t; day)

The `WEEKNUM` function is used to convert a date given in any recognizable format into the appropriate week number. You need to specify the first day of the week using an integer number (Sunday is 1, Monday is 2). For example:

```
=WEEKNUM("2/7/2010"; 0)
```

returns 5, and

```
=WEEKNUM("2/7/2010"; 1)
```

returns 6.

	A	B	C
433	MONTH	Date	Result
434	MONTH	40179	1

*Figure 12.8: Sample result of the **MONTH** function.*

Extract Month from a Date (MONTH)

Syntax: MONTH(t)

The `MONTH` function is used to convert a date given in any recognizable format into the month number. For example:

```
=MONTH(DATE(2010; 6; 27))
```

returns 6.

You can give `MONTH` the date in a more natural format, e.g.:

```
=MONTH("3/17/2010")
```

returns 3 (March 17, 2010).

See the description of the `DATE` (page 122) function for another example of using the `MONTH` function in practice.

Extract Year from a Date (YEAR)

Syntax: YEAR(t)

The `YEAR` function is used to convert a date given in any recognizable format into a year number. For example:

```
=YEAR(DATE(2010; 11; 1))
```

returns 2010.

	A	B	C
436	YEAR	Date	Result
437	YEAR	03/17/10	2010

*Figure 12.9: Sample result of the **YEAR** function.*

You can give MONTH the date in a more natural format, e.g.:

`=YEAR("3/17/2010")`

returns 2010 (March 17, 2010).

See the description of the DATE (page 122) function for another example of using it.

	A	B	C
439	DAYSINMONTH	Date	Result
440	DAYSINMONTH	02/16/12	29

*Figure 12.10: Sample result of the **DAYSINMONTH** function.*

Number of Days in a Month (DAYSINMONTH)

Syntax: DAYSINMONTH(t)

The DAYSINMONTH function returns the number of days in the given date. For example:

`=DAYSINMONTH(DATE(2012; 2; 16))`

returns 29 (February 2012 has 29 days, because the year 2012 is a leap year).

You can give MONTH the date in a more natural format, e.g.:

	A	B	C
442	DAYSINYEAR	Date	Result
443	DAYSINYEAR	02/16/12	366

*Figure 12.11: Sample result of the **DAYSINYEAR** function.*

```
=DAYSINMONTH("2/16/2012")
```

returns 29 again.

Number of Days in a Year (DAYSINYEAR)

Syntax: DAYSINYEAR(t)

The `DAYSINYEAR` function returns the number of days in the given date. For example:

```
=DAYSINYEAR(DATE(2012; 2; 16))
```

returns 366 (because the year 2010 is a leap year).

You can give `DAYSINYEAR` the date in a more natural format, e.g.:

```
=DAYSINYEAR("2/16/2012")
```

returns 366 again.

	A	B	C
445	WEEKSINYEAR	Date	Result
446	WEEKSINYEAR	02/16/12	52

Figure 12.13: Sample result of the ***FACT*** *function.*

Number of Weeks in a Year (WEEKSINYEAR)

Syntax: WEEKSINYEAR(t)

The `WEEKSINYEAR` function returns the number of weeks in the given date. For example:

```
=WEEKSINYEAR(DATE(2012; 2; 16))
```

returns 52.

You can give `WEEKSINYEAR` the date in a more natural format, e.g.:

```
=WEEKSINYEAR("2/16/2012")
```

returns 52 again.

Functions that Calculate the Difference Between Two Dates

Another handy set of functions are those that calculate the difference between two dates, which is often used to compute interest or discount in financial calculations.

	A	B	C	D
448	DAYS	Day1	Day2	Result
449	DAYS	12/15/10	12/16/09	363.87

*Figure 12.14: Sample result of the **FACT** function.*

Difference Between Two Dates in Real Units (DAYS)

Syntax: DAYS(t1; t2)

The `DAYS` function calculates the number of days between two dates. For example:

```
=DAYS("12/15/2010"; NOW())
```

returned `-383.93`. on Nov 26, 2009 at 1:35 am.

You can give `DAYSINYEAR` the date in a more natural format, e.g.:

```
=DAYS(DATE(2010; 12; 15); NOW())
```

The minus sign appears in the result because OpenOffice.org Calc always subtracts `t2` from `t1` (`t1 - t2`).

Remember that you can remove the minus sign with the `ABS` function, but you need to watch out for errors that such shortcuts may introduce to your calculations:

```
=ABS(DAYS("12/15/2010"; NOW()))
```

The `DAYS` function is useful for calculating short-term interest when money is borrowed for days rather than months or years.

It is important to remember that these calculations are based on a calendar year with 365 or 366 days (leap years).

See also the description of the `DAYS360` function.

	A	B	C	D
451	DAYS360	Day1	Day2	Year Type
452	DAYS360	01/15/10	06/01/10	0
453				
454	Result			
455	136			

Figure 12.15: Sample result of the ***DAYS360*** *function.*

Difference Between Two Dates in Banker's Units (DAYS360)

Syntax: DAYS360(t1; t2; year_type)

The DAYS360 function calculates the number of days between two dates given as timestamps, in bankers years. For example:

```
=DAYS360(DATE(2010; 1; 15); DATE(2010; 6; 1); 0)
```

returns 136.

You can give DAYS360 the date in a more natural format, e.g.:

```
=DAYS360("1/15/2010"; "6/1/2010"; 0)
```

The bankers year has 12 months of 30 days each giving a total of 360 days in a year. It was, and sometimes still is, used before banks started using computers. It simplifies calculations when they are done by hand, but is not fair to the banks or the borrowers.

The last number in the DAYS360 function ought to be 0 or 1, depending on which, European (1) or American (0), kind of 360-day year you want to use.

If you need to use the DAYS360 function, always make sure that you choose the right system.

See also the description of the DAYS function on page 131.

	A	B	C	D
457	MONTHS	Day1	Day2	Month Type
458	MONTHS	01/15/10	02/01/10	0
459				
460	Result			
461	0			

*Figure 12.16: Sample result of the **MONTHS** function.*

Number of Months Between Two Dates (MONTHS)

Syntax: MONTHS(t1; t2)

The `MONTHS` function calculates the number of months between two dates, either in monthly intervals (0) or calendar months (1). For example:

```
=MONTHS(DATE(2010; 1; 15); DATE(2010; 2; 1); 0)
```

returns 0, because the difference between these two dates is less than the length of one full month, and

```
=MONTHS(DATE(2010; 1; 15); DATE(2010; 2; 1); 1)
```

returns 1, because in "calendar" terms, there is a difference of one month (in February, we think of January 15 as last month's date).

You can give `MONTHS` the date in a more natural format, e.g.:

```
=MONTHS("1/15/2010"; "2/1/2010"; 0)
```

	A	B	C	D
463	WEEKS	Day1	Day2	Week Type
464	WEEKS	01/15/10	02/01/10	0
465				
466	Result			
467	2			

*Figure 12.17: Sample result of the **WEEKS** function.*

Number of Months Between Two Dates (WEEKS)

Syntax: WEEKS(t1; t2; week_type)

The WEEKS function calculates the number of weeks between two dates, either in weekly intervals (0) or calendar weeks (1). For example:

```
=WEEKS(DATE(2010; 1; 15); DATE(2010; 2; 1); 0)
```

returns 2, because the difference between these two dates is less than the length of three full weeks (21 days), and

```
=WEEKS(DATE(2010; 1; 15); DATE(2010; 2; 1); 1)
```

returns 3, because in "calendar" terms, in February we think of January 15 as being three weeks ago.

You can give WEEKS the date in a more natural format, e.g.:

```
=WEEKS("1/15/2010"; "2/1/2010"; 0)
```

	A	B	C	D
469	YEARS	Day1	Day2	Year Type
470	YEARS	12/31/09	01/01/10	0
471				
472	Result			
473	0			

*Figure 12.18: Sample results of the **YEARS** function.*

Number of Months Between Two Dates (YEARS)

Syntax: YEARS(t1; t2; year_type)

The YEARS function calculates the number of years between two dates, either in yearly intervals (0) or calendar years (1). For example:

```
=YEARS(DATE(2009; 12; 31); DATE(2010; 1; 1); 0)
```

returns 0, because the difference between these two dates is less than the length of a full year, and

```
=YEARS(DATE(2009; 12; 31); DATE(2010; 1; 1); 1)
```

returns 1, because in "calendar" terms, there is a difference of one year between those two dates.

You can give YEARS the date in a more natural format, e.g.:

```
=YEARS("12/31/2010"; "1/1/2010"; 0)
```

All of these functions may or may not be influenced by the Epoch setting. They are affected if you mix dates from different worksheets with different Epochs and enter or reference timestamps directly into a function or formula, such as `WEEKDAY(36526; 1)`. To prevent this from happening, use the `DAY` function to provide correct timestamps.

Chapter 13

Conditional Functions

All of the functions discussed in the previous chapters of this book work in a fairly simple way. You give them some input, they process it and return a single value. Useful, but not what we would call "smart."

If you want your worksheets to be a little smarter you need to use conditional functions that can make decisions based on a set of pre-defined conditions.

One good example of the need for a worksheet to be smart are tax returns. Let's assume that we want to use just two cells in a sheet, one to enter the amount of money to be taxed and the other to display the amount of tax due, using the following imaginary income tax rates:

- a tax-free allowance of $5,000.
- 20% tax on any amount above $5,000.
- 30% tax on any amount above $20,000.

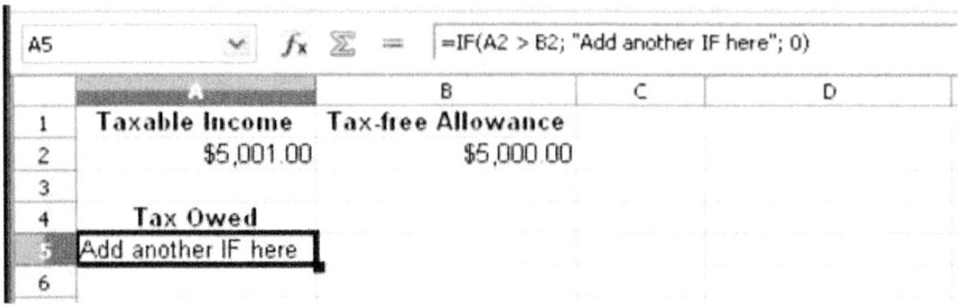

Figure 13.1: Testing for the tax-free allowance.

What you need to compute the correct amount of tax is a formula that can make decisions based on the amount of taxable income. If you were to explain them to somebody, you would say:

- *If the amount of taxable income is $5,000 or less, there is no tax to pay.*
- *If the amount of taxable income is greater than $5,000 but not greater than $20,000, subtract $5,000 from the amount of taxable income. The income tax payable on the remaining amount of taxable income is 20%.*
- *If the amount of taxable income is greater than $20,000, subtract $20,000 from the amount of taxable income. The income tax payable on the remaining amount of taxable income is 30% + $3,000.*

As you can see, even a fairly simple set of rules like the ones given on the previous page can take quite a few sentences to explain. That can be problematic for computers, because they like short, precise instructions.

Fortunately, there is a way to describe various conditions in a simple, terse format using the `IF` function and a set of relational operators discussed in the following sections of this chapter.

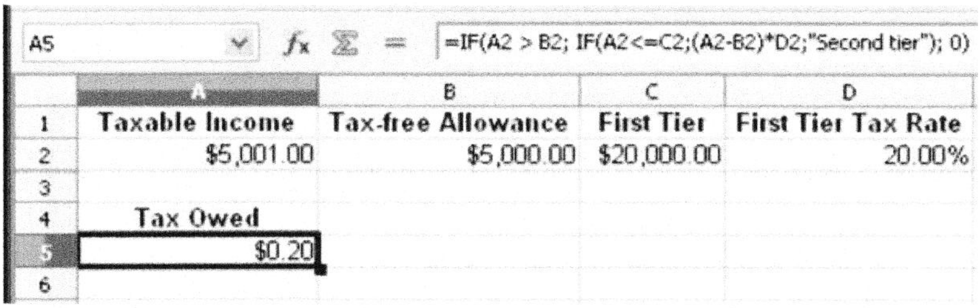

Figure 13.2: Testing for the first tax tier.

Making Decisions (IF)

Syntax: IF(test; true; false)

The most important of all conditional functions used in OpenOffice.org Calc is IF. It takes three arguments:

- `test` — the condition you want to test for.
- `true` — what IF returns when `test` returns TRUE.
- `false` — what IF returns when `test` returns FALSE.

In the case of the tax rates mentioned on the previous page, you need to build a nested formula that uses more than one IF function. Let's do it one step at a time.

The first condition is for the $5,000 exemption. Put the taxable income into cell A2 and the tax-free allowance into cell B2. The formula will look like the one below and in Figure 13.1 and you can put it anywhere, but for the purpose of this exercise it will be cell A5:

```
=IF(A2 > B2; "Add another IF here"; 0)
```

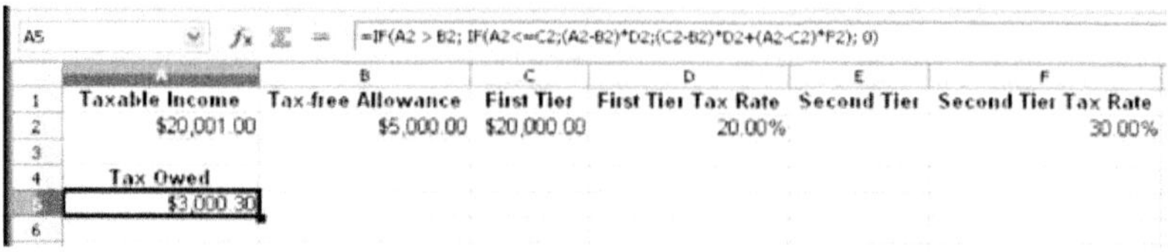

Figure 13.3: Testing for the second tax tier.

The text that appears in cell A5 after you enter a number greater that the tax-free allowance stored in cell B2 needs to be replaced with another test implemented as a nested IF function. In such case, you drop the = sign from the front of the nested function. You will now add the first taxable income tier and rate and implement it in the following way:

```
=IF(A2 > B2;
        IF(A2 <= C2; (A2-B2)*D2; "Second tier");
        0)
```

Because you cannot use multiline formulas in OpenOffice.org Calc, you need to enter the new formula into cell A5 in the following way:

```
=IF(A2 > B2; IF(A2 <= C2; (A2-B2)*D2; "Second
tier"); 0)
```

As you can see, there is a placeholder for the values of taxable income greater than the value stored in cell C2 (first tier) and there will go another formula for taxable income greater that $20,000:

```
=IF(A2 > B2;
        IF(A2 <= C2;
                (A2-B2)*D2;
                (C2-B2)*D2+(A2-C2)*F2);
        0)
```

That formula too has to be typed as a single line of text into cell A5:

```
=IF(A2 > B2; IF(A2 <= C2; (A2-B2)*D2; (C2-B2)*D2+
(A2-C2)*F2); 0)
```

As you can see in Figure 13.3 there is another cell (E2) not used in this formula. It is there in case you need to add another tax tier.

Please note that the example given in this section is not based on any particular tax code. Check your local tax code for guidance on tax rates, tax tiers, and ways of computing taxes.

Relational Operators

Relational operators are used inside the `IF` function to compare two values. They represent six basic tests that can be employed to construct a conditional formula.

The following examples show formulas that display the first text string if a condition is met, or the second string if the condition is not met.

- **Equal**: `=` — A1 and A2 are equal:

  ```
  =IF(A1=A2; "A1 is equal to A2"; "A1 and A2 not
  equal")
  ```

- **Less than**: `<` — A1 is less than A2:

  ```
  =IF(A1<A2; "A1 is less than A2"; "A1 in not
  less than A2")
  ```

- **Greater than**: `>` — A1 is greater than A2:

  ```
  =IF(A1>A2; "A1 is greater than A2"; "A1 in not
  greater than A2")
  ```

- **Less than or equal to**: `<=` — A1 is less than or equal to A2:

  ```
  =IF(A1<=A2; "A1 is less than or equal to A2";
  "A1 is not less than or equal to A2")
  ```

- **Greater than or equal to**: `>=` A1 is greater than or equal to A2:

	A	B	C	D
475	AND	ARG1	ARG2	ARG3
476	AND	TRUE	TRUE	TRUE
477				
478	Result			
479	TRUE			
480				
481	AND	ARG1	ARG2	ARG3
482	AND	TRUE	FALSE	TRUE
483				
484	Result			
485	FALSE			

*Figure 13.4: Sample results of the **AND** function.*

```
=IF(A1>=A2; "A1 is greater or equal to A2";
"A1 is not greater than or equal to A2")
```

- **Different from**: <> A1 is not equal to A2:

```
=IF(A1>=A2; "A1 is different than A2"; "A1 is
not different than A2")
```

Logical Functions

Logical functions can be used to build long and complex conditional formulas where more than one test is required.

AND

Syntax: AND(cond_1; cond_2; ... cond_30)

This function is used to compare results of up to 30 (thirty) conditions. The value of AND is TRUE if *all* of the conditions tested are TRUE as well. For example, the following formula is TRUE only if A1 is equal to A2 and A3, otherwise, it is FALSE:

```
=AND(A1=A2; A2=A3)
```

	A	B	C
487	NOT	Value	Result
488	NOT	TRUE	FALSE
489	NOT	FALSE	TRUE

Figure 13.5: Sample results of the ***NOT*** *function.*

FALSE

Syntax: FALSE()

This function returns the logical value of FALSE.

See also the section on the TRUE function on page 144.

NOT

Syntax: NOT(logic_value)

NOT negates logical values, so FALSE becomes TRUE and TRUE becomes FALSE, as in these examples:

```
=NOT(1<>1)
```

returns TRUE, and

```
=NOT(1=1)
```

returns FALSE.

	A	B	C	D
491	OR	ARG1	ARG2	ARG3
492	OR	TRUE	TRUE	TRUE
493				
494	Result			
495	TRUE			
496				
497	OR	ARG1	ARG2	ARG3
498	OR	TRUE	FALSE	TRUE
499				
500	Result			
501	TRUE			

Figure 13.6: Sample results of the ***OR*** *function.*

OR

Syntax: OR(cond_1; cond_2; ... cond_30)

The OR function is used to compare results of up to 30 (thirty) conditions. The value of OR is TRUE if at least one of the conditions tested is TRUE. For example, the following formula

```
=OR(A1=A2; A2=A3)
```

is TRUE if A1 is equal to A2, if A2 is equal to A3, or if A1 is equal to A2 and A3. If A1 is not equal to A2, and A2 is not equal to A3, the formula is FALSE.

TRUE

Syntax: TRUE()

The TRUE function returns logical value of TRUE.

See also the section on the FALSE function on page 143.

Printed in Dunstable, United Kingdom

90153932R00099